JAGUAR

AN ILLUSTRATED HISTORY

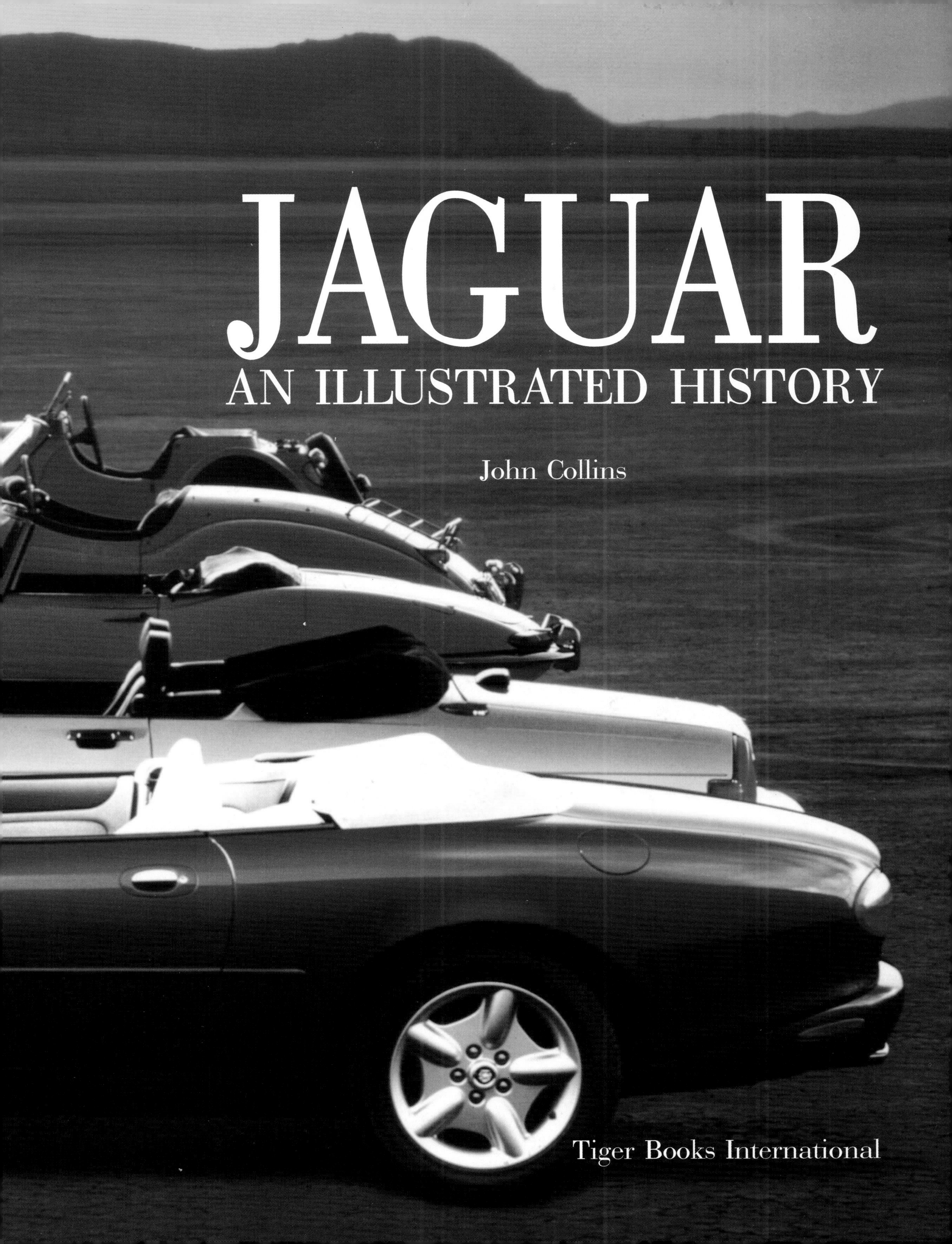

JAGUAR

AN ILLUSTRATED HISTORY

John Collins

Tiger Books International

This edition published in 1998 by
Tiger Books International PLC
Twickenham

Printed and bound by Brepols nv/sa, Belgium

ISBN 1-85501-973-6

The publishers would like to thank the Jaguar Daimler Heritage Trust for their generous assistance in supplying the pictures for this book.

Contents

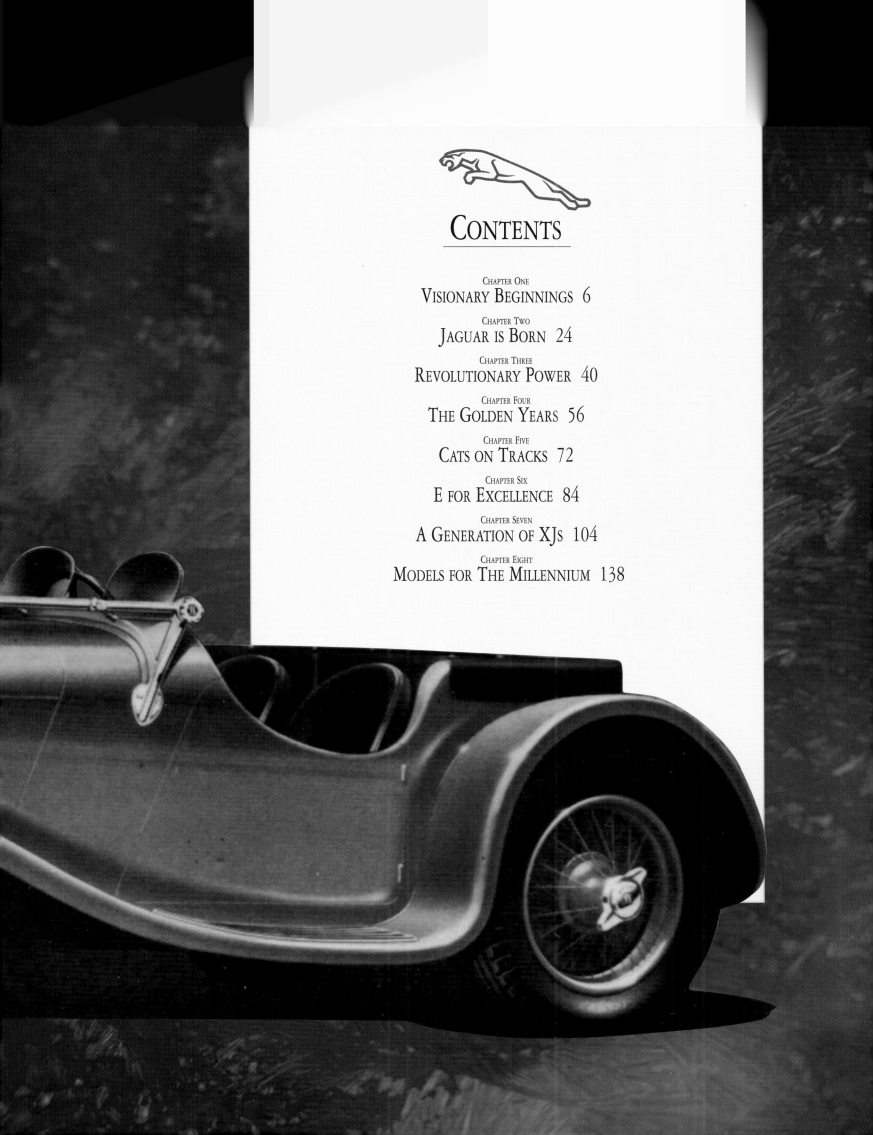

Manufacturers of
SIDE CARS & LIGHT

Chapter One

Visionary Beginnings

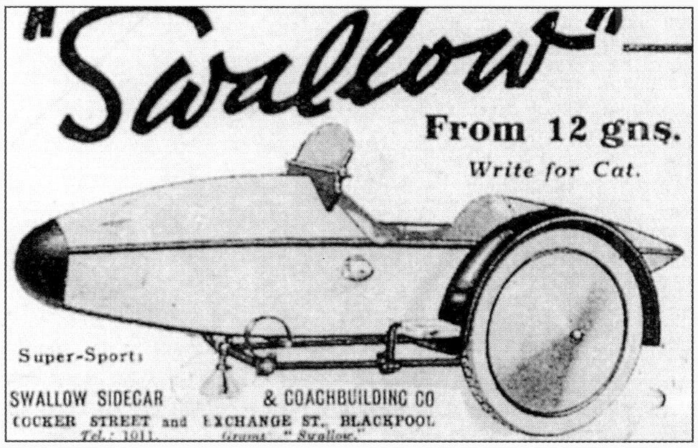

The absorbing history of Jaguar, a company with a pedigree spanning almost 80 years, had a modest introduction in the northern seaside town of Blackpool, and was born from a meeting between William Lyons, a 20-year-old with a passionate interest in motorcycles and cars, and William Walmsley, a 29-year-old who reconditioned surplus Triumph motorcycles before adding stylish sidecars of his own design.

Lyons, who had for a time found employment as an apprentice with a local garage, was fascinated by Walmsley's activities, and in 1921 he bought a sidecar from Walmsley for his own Harley-Davidson machine. In the early 1920s, before the concept of 'the motoring public' or the advent of cheap mass-produced cars, motorcycle 'combinations' were an extremely popular form of transport.

Having moved only recently from Stockport to the relative peace of the Lancashire coast, Walmsley was quite content to produce one motorcycle combination per week, but Lyons – an ambitious young man who combined a shrewd head for business with a talent for visual style – identified a good commercial opportunity if Walmsley's enterprise could be organized on a sound financial and production basis. Initially Walmsley did not share Lyons' enthusiasm, but with assets of £1,000 and financial support from both men's families, the Swallow Sidecar Company was established on 4 September 1922, the date of Lyons' twenty-first birthday.

Even before the company was formed, however, a lease had been taken on the first and second floors of a small industrial building in Bloomfield

This 'combination' of Swallow Bullet sidecar and Brough Superior motorcycle is a superb example of the stylish and immaculate work that was produced by the Swallow Sidecar Company.

From Garage to Factory

Before he met Billy Lyons, William Walmsley was quite content to produce sidecars in the garage and front room of his house in Blackpool, but Lyons had his sights set higher when the two men went into partnership in 1923. Initially they acquired premises comprising the first and second floors of a small industrial building in Bloomfield Street, Blackpool, but rapid success soon led to the acquisition of additional premises at Back Woodfield Road and John Street. Operating from three diverse premises proved to be unsatisfactory and inefficient, however, particularly as the chassis and heavy components had to be hauled to the upper floors at Bloomfield Street.

The company moved to one centralized site at Cocker Street in 1926, but very shortly thereafter it became clear that the runaway success of the Austin Swallow, combined with the continuing popularity of the sidecar, would necessitate a move to even larger premises.

The centre of the motor industry was in the Midlands, and Swallow had already advertised for skilled labour in that area due to the shortage of suitable manpower in the north-west. This fact, allied to the carriage costs involved in moving components and chassis from the Midlands to Blackpool, led the partners to search for suitable premises in the Coventry area.

In 1928, the Swallow Sidecar and Coachbuilding Company moved to a neglected former ammunition factory in the Foleshill district of Coventry, affording the company five times as much space as the Cocker Street premises. Production soon increased to 50 vehicles per week, and by the following year Swallow had acquired the adjoining factory, and doubled their production capacity yet again.

Dichotomy at Foleshill as wooden frames are prepared for sidecars (left) whilst finishing touches are made to Austin Swallows (below).

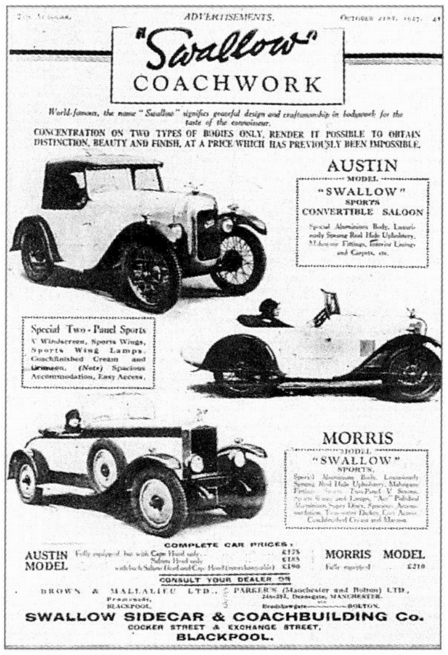

'Swallow' coachwork: a proud name heads an early advertisement for the company's range.

The SS initials were never satisfactorily explained, but 'Standard Special' and 'Swallow Sidecar' were contemporary suggestions.

Street, Blackpool. The minimum number of staff was employed, including 17-year-old Arthur Whittaker, who was to progress through the company to become Deputy Chairman in 1961, a position he held until his retirement in 1968 after 45 years of loyal service.

The new company flourished despite the economic slump of the period and manufactured several different types of sidecar, each of which could be attached to various makes and styles of motorcycle, and business expanded sufficiently to enable the company to acquire additional premises in Back Woodfield Road and John Street. Indeed, Swallow had assumed a standing of sufficient importance to allow it to exhibit at the Motor Cycle Show at Olympia in 1923, a very worthwhile exercise that resulted in the establishment of a chain of Swallow dealerships.

In 1926 the company's continuing prosperity led to its move to larger centralized premises in Cocker Street, Blackpool. This transition was soon accompanied by another, however, when the partners made the significant decision to diversify from sidecar production (that attracted only seasonal sales) to car body production (for which there was all-year-round demand).

ABOVE William Lyons was very impressed with his own Austin Seven, and Swallow bought an Austin chassis from Parkers of Bolton and Manchester on which to build its first prototype.

TOP RIGHT The Austin Seven 'Chummy' Tourer was an economical and popular car that brought affordable motoring to the masses.

To reflect this new direction in business, the Swallow Sidecar Company was renamed the Swallow Sidecar and Coachbuilding Company.

The Bullnose Morris and the Austin Seven, which was the English equivalent of the Model T Ford, had become affordable and popular forms of transport not only for the fortunate few, and were favoured by their occupants for the privilege of protection against the elements. Lyons himself had bought an Austin Seven in 1924 and was very impressed by its practicality. He commented: 'the conception of this car had a strong appeal, except that the body was a very stark affair, albeit very practical. I believe it would appeal to a lot of people if it had a more luxurious and attractive body'. Putting words into action, Lyons approached Parkers of Bolton and Manchester to sell him an Austin chassis on which the Swallow Sidecar and Coachbuilding Company could assemble a prototype. In need of assistance in this new venture, the company hired Cyril Holland, a coachbuilder from the Midlands, to impart his knowledge and expertise.

Known as the Austin Swallow Two-Seater, the stylish model was introduced in 1927 and was available in the body styles of a drophead coupé and a fixed head coupé. The Swallow's bodywork was distinctive through the use of heavy-gauge aluminium panels over a more traditional ash frame and wooden floor, and the model featured an enchanting 'wasp' tail. On early production models the hard-top was hinged to facilitate access into what was a very small car. Bodywork was customarily finished in novel, bright colour combinations such as crimson and cream, in preference to the utilitarian black or dark browns and greens that were so prevalent at the time. Attention to detail was a hallmark of the Swallow styling, manifested in such indulgencies as a Houbigant ladies companion set, the provision of which also served as an acknowledgment of the increasing number of women drivers who would be attracted to the stylish, reliable, easy-to-drive Austin Swallow, a distinctive and inexpensive luxury car that could be bought for as little as £165.

At the end of the year a larger Swallow was introduced, based on a Morris Cowley chassis and with a 1550cc engine. This model was also a two-seater and featured a rear dickey seat. Available for £220 (with wire wheels) or

£210 (without), very few examples were produced. Sidecar production also continued to expand during this period, with the company now producing 15 distinctive models and assembling up to 100 units per week.

Two years after Swallow had moved into the Cocker Street site, brisk sales continued and two significant orders were received, one from P. J. Evans Limited of Birmingham for 50 cars, the other from Henly's of London for 500 vehicles. Following this considerable order Henly's gained the sole rights for distribution in southern England.

Whilst receiving such orders was a filip for the company, expediting them was another matter, and one that Swallow found increasingly difficult in its existing premises: there was a desperate shortage of space on both the storage and manufacturing sides, and the production line was capable of producing only two cars each day. Adding to such practical difficulties was a chronic shortage of sufficiently skilled labour in the area and, on the logistical front, consideration of the high cost of transporting chassis and other raw materials from the Midlands to Blackpool. The partners realized

that another move to bigger premises was inevitable, and the company was forced to search for a larger site in the Midlands.

In 1928 the Swallow Sidecar and Coachbuilding Company moved from its birthplace and humble beginning in Blackpool to a 40,000sq ft factory at Foleshill in Coventry, the heart of Britain's motor industry and the area from which most of Swallow's supplies originated. To accompany this move Swallow decided that the time was right for another change of name, and became known as the Swallow Coachbuilding Company. Although sidecars were still being manufactured, the new identity hinted at the increasing importance and aspirations of the coachbuilding side of the business, and not long after relocation a saloon version of the Austin Two-Seater was being manufactured at the rate of 50 cars per week.

Swallow was now offering many types of body styles, especially sporting two-seaters, drophead coupés and saloons, but a larger vehicle was needed to supplement the range. As a result an Alvis conversion was produced as a prototype in 1928, and in the following year the company bought a

ABOVE Another example of the Swallow treatment is evidenced in this saloon model.

LEFT The Austin Swallow Two-Seater was introduced in 1927. The bodywork comprised aluminium panels over an ash frame and featured the delightful 'wasp' tail. Bright colour combinations were used in preference to the darker utilitarian colours applied by other manufacturers.

William Lyons

Born in September 1901 in Blackpool, where his father had founded a school of music, William Lyons was educated at the local grammar school and then at a private school before attending Manchester Technical College to read engineering. Later, after a short time at Crossley Motors, he joined his father's piano repair business for a while and then became a car salesman with both Jackson Brothers and Brown & Mallalieu in Blackpool.

The Swallow Sidecar Company resulted from a meeting between Lyons and William Walmsley in 1921, when Lyons purchased one of Walmsley's sidecars for his Harley-Davidson motorcycle.

Billy Lyons was a shrewd, ambitious man who is remembered as an autocratic and determined leader. He was also depicted as a hard taskmaster who lacked a sense of humour, but one who evidently inspired loyalty in his employees as many of them remained with the company for most of their working lives.

Reporting on the success of the Jaguar racing team at Le Mans in 1953, the Sunday Times commented: 'The man who built the team is W. Lyons, who is only 52 ... he directs it with a sustained and compelling intensity of purpose ... Physically trim and immaculate in dress, he has the aura of power but not its trappings. No entourage of secretaries and personal assistants trails his unceasing movement around the great modern factory the firm moved into 18 months ago ...'

His genius was rewarded by a knighthood in 1956, and during his working life he was appointed President of the Society of Motor Manufacturers and was also awarded the accolade of Royal Designer to Industry. He died in 1985 after a lifetime's distinguished service to the motor industry.

number of FIAT 509A chassis, on which between 50 and 100 FIAT Swallows were manufactured. Additionally, coachwork was undertaken on the Swift Ten and the Standard Big Nine, both models being exhibited at the 1929 Motor Show. The association between the Standard Motor Company and Swallow was to be a long and profitable one.

Up to 1931 Swallow had concentrated on custom-built bodies over a number of readily available chassis from other car manufacturers, and although the cars had a sporty image their appearance was not backed up by performance. This situation was addressed, however, when Lyons and Walmsley turned their attentions to the Standard Ensign. Impressed by its 15hp six-cylinder engine, they decided that such a vehicle would definitely enhance their range, and the 2054cc Standard Ensign Swallow was launched with over 50 models being produced. In the same year William Lyons reached agreement with the Standard Motor Company to produce and sell to him an exclusive version of the Standard chassis with the Standard six-cylinder engine, thus giving Lyons more control over the performance of his designs and earmarking Swallow as car manufacturers in their own right.

The purchase of the Standard chassis and six-cylinder engine available exclusively to Swallow was the basis for Lyons' first original vehicle and was indeed a landmark in the history of the company. This exciting new venture was attended by widespread advertising that proclaimed: 'WAIT! The "SS" is coming. S.S. is the new name of a new car that's going to thrill the hearts of the motoring public and the trade alike. It's something utterly new ... different ... better! Long ... low ... very low ... and very FAST!' And different it certainly was. Lyons had designed a striking body with a low and distinctive profile that was achieved by mounting the road-springs along rather than below the chassis. Other conspicuous features included a fabric-covered roof, and a boot with a top-opening lid accommodating an outside spare wheel and tyre. The Standard chassis had undergone many modifications, the wheelbase having been extended by three inches, and the

OPPOSITE By the end of the 1920s Swallow was offering a variety of body styles, and a small number of Swallows based on a FIAT chassis appeared in 1929.

ABOVE This Swallow version of the Morris Cowley chassis was introduced in 1927 and had a dickey (or rumble) seat in the tail.

ABOVE Demand for the S.S.I was constant despite the economic strictures of the 1930s. Here, S.S.I models are on display in the United States.

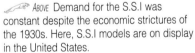

RIGHT The first Wolseley Hornet was unveiled as a two-seater in 1930 and later as a four-seater. Brisk and stylish, it was Swallow's nearest thing to a sports car.

Arthur Whittaker

Arthur Whittaker joined the formative company at the age of 17, shortly before the 1923 Motor Cycle Show, and was initially involved on the sales side of the business. Displaying an adroitness almost unbecoming for someone so young, he progressed quickly and was soon appointed buyer of components. His astute purchasing abilities enabled Lyons to offer the remarkable value for money which contributed to the lasting success of the company.

Whittaker was awarded a directorship in 1935 when S.S. Cars became a public company, and in 1961 Lyons appointed him Deputy Chairman, a position he held for seven years until his retirement in 1968.

The long, low bonnet was a distinctive feature of the S.S.I range and was considered gauche and distasteful in some quarters. The new chassis was both designed and produced exclusively for Swallow. Over 500 examples were manufactured in 1932.

Early Dealers and Exports

After having established the Swallow Sidecar Company in 1922, William Lyons very quickly recognized the vital need to appoint selling agents both in Britain and abroad. Parkers of Bolton and Manchester, the suppliers of the first chassis obtained for Swallow conversion, were appointed to oversee their own region, whilst Brown and Mallalieu (Lyons' former employers) covered Blackpool. In 1928 Lyons met with the managing directors of P.J. Evans Limited in Birmingham, who subsequently placed an order for 50 cars, and shortly after this he made arrangements with the directors of Henly's of London for that company's sole rights to distribute Swallow cars in southern England.

Meanwhile, Lyons had discussions with Swiss businessman Emil Frey at the 1926 Olympia Show. Both men shared an ardent enthusiasm for motorcycles, Frey also racing motorcycles in his own country. Their meeting resulted in an order for 20 sidecars.

Frey gained the exclusive rights for dealership in Switzerland for both sidecars and future products of the Swallow company, an agreement which formed the basis of his own extraordinarily successful garage business and which cemented a partnership between Lyons and Frey that was to continue for many decades.

Other agencies were established throughout Europe during the formative years of Swallow manufacture. Further afield, cars were supplied to Egypt, India, Palestine, Australia, Morocco, Jamaica, Madeira and Poland. In the United States, Swallow was represented by British Motors in New York County. Swallow's success worldwide not only engendered welcome profits for the company but also helped to attract much-needed foreign currency.

Hurriedly designed and built, the S.S.I was completed just in time for its debut at the Olympia Show of 1931. Described as the car with 'the £1,000 look', early models were criticized for their performance but were gradually modified and always represented good value for money.

engine moved rearwards in order to facilitate an abnormally long bonnet. Although the new range was identified by the initials 'S.S.', a definitive translation of these letters has never been forthcoming, although Standard Swallow, Swallow Sports, Swallow Sidecars, and Standard Special were all suggested possibilities.

The S.S.I cars were exhibited for the first time at the Olympia Show of 1931 and received sensational acclaim, such enthusiasm also extending to the price of just over £300. The S.S.I model was available as a long and low fixed head coupé, with the option of a six-cylinder 16hp 2054cc engine or, later, a 20hp side-valve 2552cc engine. Supplementing the S.S.I was the smaller S.S.II coupé, based on the Standard Little Nine chassis and with a four-cylinder 1066cc engine. This model was available at the even more attractive price of £210. Such exceptionally low prices were achieved both by planning for long production runs rather than repeatedly tooling-up for different models and as a result of Arthur Whittaker's bargaining ability.

For the Olympia Show of the following year the S.S.I was extensively modified; the track was lengthened by two inches and the wheelbase extended by seven inches, thus enabling the car to become a four-seater. Other revisions included a lower roofline, alterations to the front wings, and strengthening of the rear chassis to permit adults to occupy the new rear seats and to provide more legroom.

Despite the austere economic circumstances of the 1930s, demand for S.S. models was constant, possibly because they were luxurious and distinctive vehicles at a reasonable price, and allowed people who had previously

S.S.I COUPÉ (FIRST SERIES)

MODEL	Fixed Head Coupé
ENGINE	Side-valve 6-cylinder, 2054 and 2552cc
MAX. POWER	45 and 55bhp
MAX. SPEED	70mph
PERFORMANCE	0-50 in 20 seconds (2054cc)
WEIGHT	Not available
LENGTH	Not available
WIDTH	Not available
IN PRODUCTION	1932
QUANTITY	502
PRICE	£310 and £320

S.S.I COUPÉ (SECOND SERIES)

MODEL	Fixed Head Coupé
ENGINE	Side-valve 6-cylinder, 2054 and 2552cc (1933) 2143 and 2663cc (1934)
MAX. POWER	48 and 62bhp (1933) 53 and 68bhp (1934) 62 and 70bhp (1935)
MAX. SPEED	75 and 81.8mph (1933)
PERFORMANCE	0-50 in 28.4 and 21.4 seconds (1933)
WEIGHT	Not available
LENGTH	Not available
WIDTH	Not available
IN PRODUCTION	1933-1936
QUANTITY	1,099 (1933) and 200 (1934/5)
PRICE	£325 (1933) and £335 (1934/5)

S.S.II COUPÉ (FIRST SERIES)

MODEL	Fixed Head Coupé
ENGINE	Side-valve 4-cylinder, 1006cc
MAX. POWER	28bhp
MAX. SPEED	60mph
PERFORMANCE	0-50 in 26.6 seconds
WEIGHT	Not available
LENGTH	Not available
WIDTH	Not available
IN PRODUCTION	1932-1933
QUANTITY	549
PRICE	£210

S.S.I TOURER

MODEL	Open Four-Seater
ENGINE	Side-valve 6-cylinder, 2054 and 2552cc (1933) 2143 and 2663cc (1934)
MAX. POWER	48 and 62bhp (1933) 53 and 68bhp (1934) 62 and 70bhp (1935)
MAX. SPEED	Not available
PERFORMANCE	0-50 in 23 seconds (1935 2663cc)
WEIGHT	Not available
LENGTH	Not available
WIDTH	Not available
IN PRODUCTION	1933-1934 and 1934-1936
QUANTITY	551
PRICE	£325 (2054cc), £335 (2143cc) £335 (2552cc), £340 (2663cc)

S.S.I SALOON

MODEL	Four-light Saloon
ENGINE	Side-valve 6-cylinder, 2143 and 2663cc
MAX. POWER	53 and 68bhp (1934) 62 and 70bhp (1935)
MAX. SPEED	81.5mph (1935 2663cc)
PERFORMANCE	0-60 in 24 seconds (1935 2663cc)
WEIGHT	Not available
LENGTH	Not available
WIDTH	Not available
IN PRODUCTION	1933-1936
QUANTITY	1,144
Price	£340 and £345

S.S.II COUPÉ, SALOON AND TOURER

MODELS	Fixed Head Coupé, Four-light Saloon, Open Four-Seater
ENGINE	Side-valve 4-cylinder, 1343 and 1608cc
MAX. POWER	32 and 38bhp
MAX. SPEED	61.2mph
PERFORMANCE	Not available
WEIGHT	Not available
LENGTH	Not available
WIDTH	Not available
IN PRODUCTION	Coupé and Saloon 1934-1936 Tourer 1934-1935
QUANTITY	Coupé 154, Saloon 905, Tourer 186
PRICE	Not available

S.S.I AIRLINE

MODEL	Fastback Saloon
ENGINE	Side-valve 6-cylinder, 2143 and 2663cc
MAX. POWER	62 and 70bhp
MAX. SPEED	80mph
PERFORMANCE	Not available
WEIGHT	Not available
LENGTH	Not available
WIDTH	Not available
IN PRODUCTION	1935-1936
QUANTITY	624
PRICE	£360 and £365

S.S.I DROPHEAD COUPÉ

MODEL	Folding-top Coupé
ENGINE	Side-valve 6-cylinder, 2143 and 2663cc
MAX. POWER	62 and 70bhp
MAX. SPEED	80mph
PERFORMANCE	Not available
WEIGHT	Not available
LENGTH	15ft 6in
WIDTH	5ft 5in
IN PRODUCTION	1935-1936
QUANTITY	100
PRICE	£380 and £385

S.S. 90

MODEL	Two-Seater Sports
ENGINE	Side-valve 6-cylinder, 2663cc
MAX. POWER	70bhp
MAX. SPEED	90mph
PERFORMANCE	0-60 in 17 seconds
WEIGHT	Not available
LENGTH	Not available
WIDTH	Not available
IN PRODUCTION	1935-1936
QUANTITY	24
PRICE	£395

owned a more expensive car to 'keep up appearances'. By 1933, for example, production of the S.S.I was running at about 1,100 vehicles annually. Popularity of the S.S. series dictated that production of other Swallow-bodied vehicles was scaled down in 1932 and ended in 1933, when both the S.S.I and S.S.II ranges were enhanced to include tourers and, in the following year, saloons. The four-seat open Tourer, featuring a side-valve six-cylinder engine, was available at prices ranging from £325 to £340, and about 150 examples were sold in 1933. The Saloon, which incorporated four side windows, sold at £340 or £345.

BELOW The S.S.I Tourer sold reasonably well and an S.S.II model in this form was offered in 1934 for customers who preferred something a little smaller.

Below Launched in 1935 and not a particular favourite of William Lyons, the S.S.I Airline featured a distinctive curved back, and was introduced as a rival to the Airflow manufactured by the Chrysler Corporation.

Despite the introduction of new and attractive models, detractors of the company (now known as S.S. Cars) were quick to criticise their performance, and in an effort to overcome such criticism all S.S. models were equipped with larger 2143cc or 2663cc engines and the track was increased by a further two inches. Concurrently the S.S.IIs were also improved, with 1343cc or 1606cc engines, a new chassis on a wheelbase extended by 14½ inches, and with the track extended by 1½ inches. A saloon model was soon launched, followed by the S.S.II Tourer and the spectacular Airline Saloon.

In 1934 the Chrysler Corporation of America introduced a new model, the Airflow, the exterior design of which had been formulated with the aid of a wind tunnel. This new design concept was copied by many manufacturers, including Peugeot, Volvo and Hillman, although their models had not necessarily undergone aerodynamic testing in wind tunnels. Always keen to be among the first with new designs, S.S. Cars introduced a rival in the form of the S.S.I Airline in September. Constructed of aluminium over a wood frame, this fastback saloon was not a particular favourite of William Lyons, but 624 examples were produced over the next two years. The Airline, with its distinctive curved back, was available with engine sizes of 2143cc and 2663cc, and sold for £360 and £365 respectively.

Notwithstanding the ambitious variety of new models, however, the enterprising partnership between Lyons and Walmsley was about to come to an end. Lyons was keen to expand the company against Walmsley's wishes, and at the annual general meeting of S.S. Cars in November 1934, Walmsley resigned and the partnership was dissolved. S.S. Cars became a public company in January 1935, and Lyons was appointed Chairman and Managing Director, having purchased sufficient shares to have a majority holding.

William Lyons continued the pursuit for better performance, and moved toward establishing an engineering department to further his aims. Just

Opposite Bolton Police take delivery of an S.S.I Tourer. Jaguars remain a favourite of many constabularies in Britain today.

two months after the company achieved public status, two new models in the form of the S.S.I Drophead and the S.S.90 emerged from the company's works. The Drophead was a variation of the S.S.I and incorporated a folding hood that could be retracted under a hinged tonneau behind the seats. The S.S.90 was assembled on a shortened S.S.I chassis, and with the side-valve six-cylinder 2663cc engine was capable of 90mph. The model had a small production run of 24 before being replaced by the S.S.100.

A notable name involved on engine development of the S.S.90 was Harry Weslake, a gas-flow expert who was employed by Lyons as a freelance consultant. Soon after the S.S.90's introduction in March 1935, William Heynes, another gifted engineer, was headhunted from Humber to co-ordinate the engineering department. He was to play a very significant part in the fortunes of the company for many years.

The design of the Chrysler Airflow had evolved with the aid of wind-tunnel tests and was imitated by manufacturers including Volvo, Hillman and Peugeot. Lyons reluctantly agreed to allow the Airline to be built, but only 624 examples were produced during 1935 and 1936.

Reminiscent of a bird in flight, this poignant Swallow logo was adopted in the 1930s.

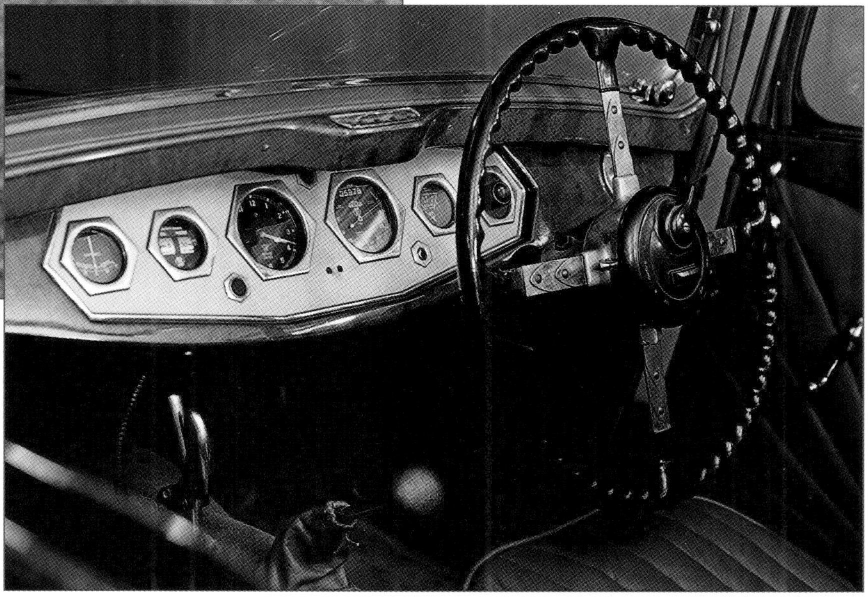

The dashboard of this S.S.II depicts the very large steering wheel and the elegant hexagonal shape of the instrument dials.

Chapter Two

Jaguar is Born

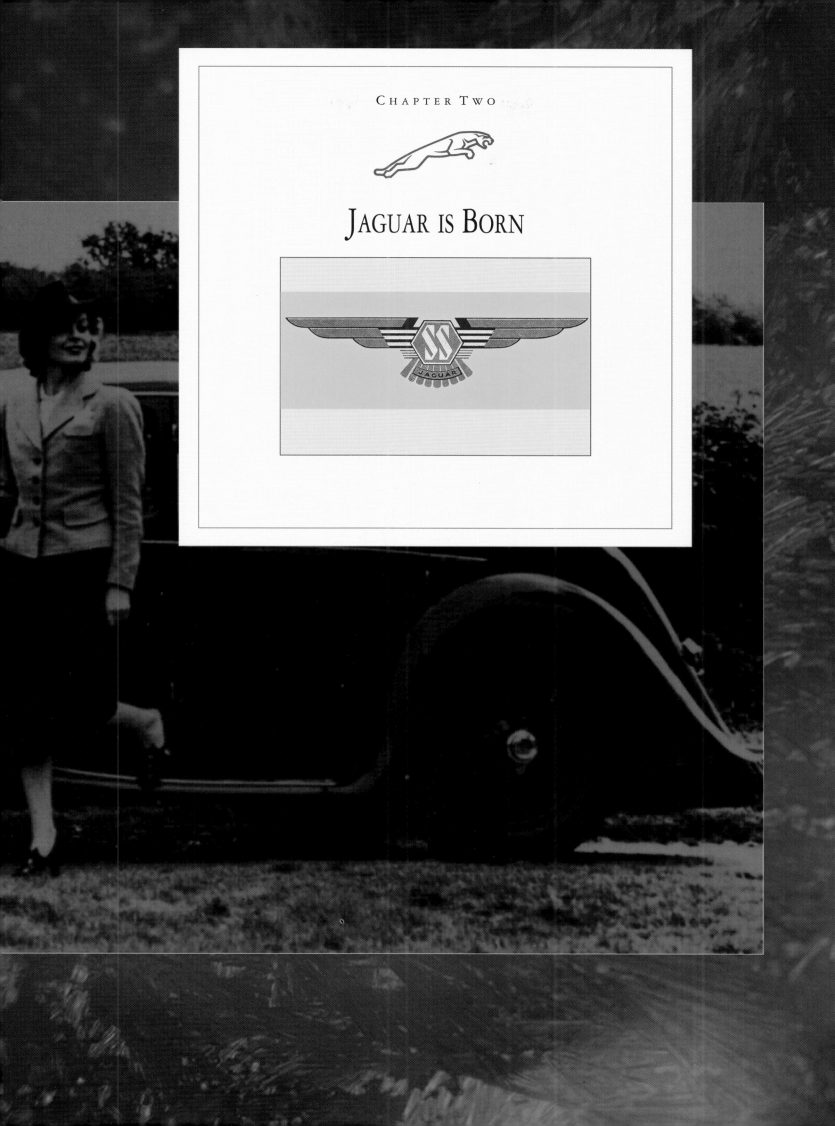

In securing the services of William Heynes, Lyons had demonstrated yet again the breadth and wisdom of his own astute foresight. The fortunes of the company and its place at the cutting edge of automotive technology hinged on the success of the new engineering department, and from this time nearly everything to emerge from that department bore the hallmarks of Heynes himself.

Soon after Heynes's appointment, Lyons was convinced that the company trade name required a sharper image. Learning that the Sunbeam Motor Company was about to be sold he made arrangements to purchase the business and hurriedly prepared for a new model range that would carry the Sunbeam monogram. However, his project was thwarted by the rival firm of Rootes Brothers, which managed to acquire the Sunbeam name before Lyons could finalize his plans.

BELOW Two enthusiasts look forward to a ride in a prototype S.S.90 that was introduced less than three months after S.S. Cars became a public company.

BOTTOM This revealing view of the S.S.90's dashboard shows the speedometer and revolution counter on a single dial.

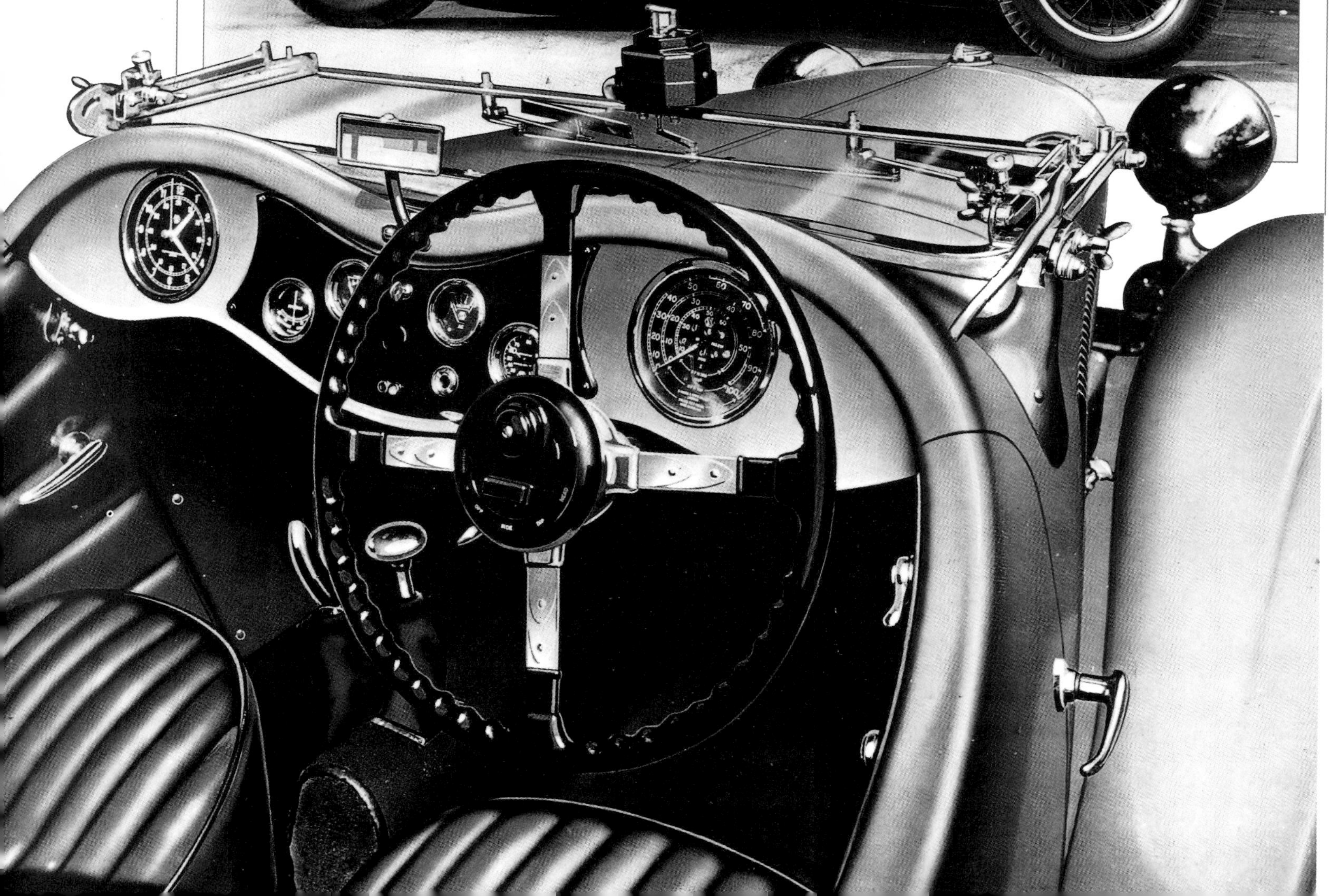

Left Although dated by the standards of the late twentieth century, this catalogue cover for the S.S. range is highly typical of the advertising style of the 1930s.

It was a matter of some importance that a new and distinctive title was found in time for the launch of the 1936 S.S. range. The company's advertising agents supplied a list of animal names, from which Lyons chose one that combined the elements of grace, strength and speed: Jaguar; and from this time all models were known as SS Jaguars. (Before being allowed to apply this signature, however, Lyons had to seek permission from Armstrong-Siddeley who were already producing an aircraft engine of the same name.)

From 1935 until the outbreak of World War II new models appeared at an impressive rate. One of Heynes's first undertakings was to modify the range for 1936, and Harry Weslake was charged with uprating the Standard six-cylinder 2½-litre engine, which he converted to overhead-valve operation. This increased its output from 75bhp to 105bhp, and after conversion a 2½-litre saloon or tourer was capable of almost 90mph.

Significantly, the new range included the company's first four-door saloon. Constructed of steel panels over an ash frame, the saloon was notable for its wider body, achieved by positioning the rear springs inside the S.S.I chassis that was itself widened and strengthened; the spare wheel was now positioned in the left-hand front wing and the model sported an impressive radiator grille. Unveiled concurrently was a 1½-litre version of the same saloon based on a shorter form of the wider, strengthened chassis. Powered by a Standard 1608cc side-valve engine, this model was contrasted by its shorter bonnet and front wings, and was distinctive for the fact that the spare wheel rose proud of the bonnet as a result of the revised bonnet styling. A Tourer, assembled on the new chassis and powered by the overhead-valve engine, was produced during 1936 and 1937 but only about 100 examples were made.

Both versions of the new saloon were introduced at the 1935 London Motor Show, but for many visitors the highlight was the unveiling of the company's first sports car, the SS100. Outwardly similar to the S.S.90 (of which only 24 were produced), the sensational SS100 promised dynamic performance: with the 2½-litre overhead-valve engine producing 102bhp, this thoroughbred was capable of 0-60 in 13 seconds and a top speed around the 95mph mark. The world's motoring press was ablaze with excitement, Motor magazine acclaiming: 'The acceleration in top gear is so very rapid that the lazy driver may retain this ratio almost indefinitely'. Also on the subject of the impressive third gear, Autocar enthused: 'a burst on this ratio for overtaking purposes sends the car shooting forward, and it is up into the 60 to 70mph range extremely rapidly'. In Weslake's engine Jaguar had found a winner, a dazzling performer that would outshine not only the cheaper sports cars from makers such as MG and Riley, but also many more-expensive examples of the breed.

By 1936 the company had entered the world of competition racing. In an SS100 the team of Bill and Elsie Wisdom achieved best individual performance in the Alpine Trial, and McEvoy recorded a class win in the Marne Sports Car Grand Prix at Reims. Sammy Newsome beat all-comers to win the 3-litre unsupercharged class event at the Shelsley Walsh meeting

LEFT With its folding hood down on a cold day, an S.S.90 awaits the return of its hale and hearty driver.

ABOVE Based on a shortened form of the S.S.I chassis, the visually exciting S.S.90 was William Lyons' first attempt at producing a sports car. Only 24 models were built, however, and examples are very rarely found today.

LEFT With Harry Weslake's six-cylinder 2663cc engine the S.S.90 was capable of 90mph, although overall performance was disappointing.

ABOVE Sporty and nimble, the 3½-litre SS100 was capable of the magic 'ton'.

ABOVE Beautiful, bold, brazen headlamps were a stunning frontal feature of the exciting SS100.

BELOW Sensational both inside and out, this photograph admirably illustrates some detail of the SS100's voluptuous interior design.

in September, and in March 1937 Jack Harrop and Bob Taylor triumphed in the RAC Rally. A works-supported car, registered BWK 77 and often known as 'Old Number Eight' after its chassis plate, achieved great success for the SS Jaguar stable in the same year: driven by Jacob it won best performance at the Welsh Rally in July, and also took Newsome to victories at Shelsley and Brooklands.

Such was the popularity of the new SS Jaguar range that demand was soon outstripping supply, and production methods at Foleshill were in urgent need of reorganization. The company's traditional production process involving ash frames and steel panels was no longer suited to the output levels required, nor could

ABOVE Awaiting a photocall, a trio of SS Jaguars recline in the sunshine.

it satisfy Lyons' constant pursuit of economy and efficiency. Regretfully, Lyons had no alternative but to sanction the conversion to all-steel panel bodywork in 1937 and, as the company itself could not produce the necessary pressings for this process, he contracted with several outside suppliers to produce the components that would then be assembled by Jaguar, and immediately increased his workforce in anticipation.

Ironically, the move that was designed to solve the problems of body production presaged a disastrous year that almost bankrupted the company. Late delivery and non-delivery of parts together with the fact that many components were ill-fitting when they did arrive resulted in a troublesome few months, and the increased workforce was idle until the situation was resolved. Jaguar received substantial compensation from some suppliers, however, and increased production heralded record profits for the company in 1938. The new all-steel models were outwardly similar to their forerunners except for their larger doors and the position of the spare wheel, which was now located in the boot-lid (and later under the boot floor): quite apart from this cosmetic enhancement, such a modification offered obvious aerodynamic advantages.

BELOW Announced in 1935, the 1½-litre version of the new Jaguar saloon was based on a shortened form of Heynes's S.S.I chassis. The spare wheel was mounted on the left-hand front wing.

William Heynes

William Heynes, a name unequivocally associated with Jaguar, was born in Leamington in 1903. Educated at Warwick School, he became an apprentice with Humber Limited from 1922 to 1925, transferring to work in the drawing office before becoming an assistant to the Chief Stress Engineer. Rootes Brothers took over the company in 1928, and it was another seven years before William Lyons approached Heynes and offered him the post of Chief Engineer with SS Jaguar.

In charge of the new engineering department, Heynes's principal task was to design a new chassis and incorporate other improvements for the new SS Jaguar range to be introduced in 1936. Indeed, Heynes was the mastermind behind every Jaguar produced after 1935, including the unitary construction of small saloons, and the chassis and engine design for the XK range and the larger saloons. Together with Malcolm Sayer, he was the brains behind the C and D Type Jaguars and also designed the classic E Type.

Heynes was a gifted engineer, and is largely responsible for Jaguar's irrefutable reputation for performance. Appointed to the Board of Directors early in 1945, Heynes was reputedly one of the few employees able to express his mind to his dictatorial boss. Heynes retired to the Warwickshire countryside having left an engaging tape-recording of his experiences in the motor industry.

The radical change in bodywork materials was accompanied by continuing improvement in engine performance: the 1½-litre engine (based on the Standard 4-cylinder 1776cc engine) received an overhead-valve conversion, thus boosting output from 45hp to 65hp, and was fitted in the four-door saloon; the 2½-litre engine's power output was raised to around 100bhp through an increased compression ratio and improved exhaust manifolding; but truly exceptional performance was provided by a new 3½-litre engine producing 125bhp, and featuring the Weslake cylinder head, two SU carburettors and two triple-branch exhaust manifolds: this unit was fitted in the SS100 to produce the first Jaguar capable of the magic 'ton'.

The 1½-, 2½- and 3½-litre Jaguars were now also available in two-door drophead coupé versions, enabling the 1938 range to boast two-door convertibles, four-door saloons, and the uprated SS100 that was exhibited in prototype streamlined form at that year's Earl's Court Show. SS100s continued to distinguish themselves in competitive racing, with a string of successes throughout the year including wins in the RAC and Welsh Rallies.

Toward the end of 1938, and only a matter of months before civilian life was thrown into turmoil by the declaration of war in September 1939, the Jaguar production line was turning out new models at the rate of 5,000 per year. Forever ambitious, Lyons was intent on continuing expansion and was working on plans for a brand new engine. With his well-established knack of finding the right man for the job, Lyons tempted Walter Hassan, formerly with Bentley and at the time a tuning 'ace' at Brooklands, and appointed him Chief Experimental Engineer. Unfortunately, engine development work was curtailed after the outbreak of World War II, and a frustrated Hassan left the company, only to return in 1943 to work on a range of special vehicles that Jaguar was developing for the war effort.

In the last few months of 1939 car production ceased. In common with many other British car manufacturers during the six years of war, the company concentrated its efforts on the building and repairing of aircraft and aircraft parts, although a certain amount of experimental work was undertaken. Jaguar was primarily involved with the manufacture of cockpit roofs, bomb doors, armaments, wings and fuselages for Lancasters,

RIGHT This 1937 four-door 2½-litre saloon was owned by Lady Lyons, and during the year of its manufacture her husband made the momentous decision to convert to all-steel panel bodywork.

Above A chauffeur shows his passenger to the front seat of a 1937 2½-litre Saloon.

Mosquitos, Spitfires and Stirlings, and the company also repaired Whitley and Wellington bombers. Toward the end of the war Jaguar produced sections for the Gloster Meteor, the first Allied jet aircraft to serve operationally in World War II.

Alongside this work the building of sidecars continued with renewed fervour. At the same time as S.S. Cars became a public company Lyons had auspiciously established Swallow Coachbuilding (1935) Ltd, a dedicated sidecar arm of the business that had quietly prospered during the intervening years but which assumed increasing importance during the war, building sidecars and trailers for the army, navy and air force as well as for the country's fire brigades.

In the company's factories the essential task of fire-watching was undertaken by employees who would operate in shifts. Never a man to

Ernest 'Bill' Rankin

After World War I Bill Rankin worked as an advertising representative for General Motors before entering and winning a design competition run by the Watney Brewery, for whom he created the legendary Red Barrel symbol.

Rankin joined SS Cars before the company had decided to change its name and, following an advertising agency's proferred list of animal names, it has been suggested that Rankin had more than a hand in the company's choice of 'Jaguar'. Whether or not that was true, he was certainly responsible for the distinctive trademark. A crude accessory version of the Jaguar cat was produced by an outside firm in 1937, Rankin describing it as "a cat shot off a fence". As an amateur sculptor, he produced his own more acceptable version which adorned the bonnets of Jaguar cars for many years.

William Lyons had many ideas, but it was Rankin who had the genius for producing bold, eye-catching advertisements in keeping with the designs and colour schemes he was aiming to sell. Eloquent testimony to his art was provided by his successor, Bob Berry, who commented: 'if it was written, printed or advertised, Rankin was responsible for it ... he was undoubtedly the guy who was responsible for the creation of the whole Jaguar image'. Rankin died in 1966.

Left Harry Weslake was in charge of uprating the Standard six-cylinder 2½-litre engine, which he converted to overhead-valve operation.

The Appleyards

Ian Appleyard was a Jaguar distributor in Leeds, and was married to Pat, one of Lyons' daughters. His love of speed had taken him to the 1948 Olympic Games where he represented Great Britain at skiing and had also turned his attention to motor rallying.

At first driving his own 1938 3½-litre SS100 he soon ran out of spare parts, and then acquired a similar model that had been stored throughout the war at Lyons' home. Appleyard triumphed many times in this vehicle, registration LNW 100, even after Jaguar had ceased production of the SS100.

Using this car, that was virtually in standard form except for improvements to the steering mechanism, Appleyard entered the 1948 Alpine Rally. Despite heavy rain and delays caused by snowdrifts as well as by the appearance on the course of an immovable herd of cows, Appleyard finished equal first with Potter, who was driving an Allard. After a short 'decider' involving tests of accelerating, reversing and braking, Appleyard finished 0.3 seconds ahead of Porter and collected the prized Coupe des Alpes.

Tourers were superseded by Drophead saloons with three engine options, and the interiors were still luxuriously appointed (above). The 2½-litre Drophead (right) was available for the amazing price of £415.

Right During World War II, Jaguar concentrated its efforts on manufacturing components for aircraft such as the Lancaster and Spitfire, as well as repairing Whitley and Wellington bombers.

shirk his duties, Lyons included himself in this mundane task and occupied his mind by planning for the future. He co-ordinated the shifts so that he could share the company of Walter Hassan, William Heynes and Claude Bailey (who had come to Jaguar just before the outbreak of war), and together they discussed and schemed for the future.

With the end of the war in 1945 military work ceased and Lyons was able to pursue his vision for the future more realistically. (Earlier that year the company had changed its name to Jaguar Cars Ltd in order to distance itself from the offensive connotations of the SS initials.) An apparent setback to that vision came when Sir John Black of Standard Cars announced that his company was investing its hopes in the Vanguard and would no longer be able to supply the 2½- and 3½-litre engines (Standard continued to supply the 1½-litre engine). Recognizing an opportunity to become an independent manufacturing unit, Lyons immediately made an offer to purchase all the tooling necessary to build the engines. The offer was accepted and, for the first time, Jaguar Cars was in the enviable position of being able to construct cars from scratch. Later, Black was to suggest restoration of the former arrangement, to which Lyons replied, 'No thank you John. I have now got the ball, and I would rather kick it myself'.

The British motor industry was only one of many manufacturing industries facing an uphill struggle in the post-war climate of petrol rationing and steel shortages. The steel quota system introduced after the war was intended to encourage exports and particularly favoured those industries that were exporting goods before 1939. Jaguar benefited significantly from this arrangement and did its utmost to further the export drive, to the extent that 35 per cent of all new production cars were exported between 1946 and 1949.

In 1946 Heynes became a member of the boardroom, and Bailey was promoted to Chief Engineer. Another notable recruit to the company was former racing mechanic F.R.W. 'Lofty' England, who was appointed Service Manager. The period after the war was essentially recuperative rather than revolutionary, and the Jaguar production line resumed although the three

S.S JAGUAR 2½ LITRE SALOON AND TOURER

MODELS	Two-door Four-Seater Saloon, Open Four-Seater
ENGINE	Overhead-valve 6-cylinder, 2663cc
MAX. POWER	102bhp
MAX. SPEED	85.7mph
PERFORMANCE	060 in 17.4 seconds
WEIGHT	Not available
LENGTH	Not available
WIDTH	Not available
IN PRODUCTION	1936-1937
QUANTITY	Saloon 3,413, Tourer 98
PRICE	£385 and £375

SS JAGUAR 1½ LITRE SALOON

MODEL	Two-door, Four-Seater saloon
ENGINE	Side-valve 4-cylinder, 1608cc
MAX. POWER	52bhp
MAX. SPEED	70mph
PERFORMANCE	0-60 in 33 seconds
WEIGHt	Not available
LENGTH	Not available
WIDTH	Not available
IN PRODUCTION	1936-1938
QUANTITY	2,208
PRICE	£285

SS JAGUAR 100

MODEL	Two-Seater Sports
ENGINE	Overhead-valve 6-cylinder, 2663 and 3485cc
MAX. POWER	102 and 125bhp
MAX. SPEED	94 and 101mph
PERFORMANCE	0-60 in 12.8 and 10.9 seconds
WEIGHT	23cwt (1938)
LENGTH	12ft 6in (1938)
WIDTH	5ft 3in (1938)
IN PRODUCTION	1936-1940 and 1938-1940
QUANTITY	198 and 116
PRICE	£395 and £445

SS JAGUAR 1½ LITRE SALOON AND DROPHEAD COUPÉ

MODELS	Four-door Saloon, Two-door Convertible (all-steel)
ENGINE	Overhead-valve 4-cylinder, 1776cc
MAX. POWER	65bhp
MAX. SPEED	71.7mph
PERFORMANCE	0-60 in 25.1 seconds
WEIGHT	Not available
LENGTH	Not available
WIDTH	Not available
IN PRODUCTION	1938-1940
QUANTITY	Saloon 4,402, Coupé 675
PRICE	Saloon £298, Coupé £318

SS JAGUAR 2½ LITRE SALOON AND DROPHEAD COUPÉ

MODELS	Four-door Saloon, Two-door Convertible (all-steel)
ENGINE	Overhead-valve 6-cylinder, 2663cc
MAX. POWER	105bhp
MAX. SPEED	87mph
PERFORMANCE	060 in 17 seconds
WEIGHT	Not available
LENGTH	Not available
WIDTH	Not available
IN PRODUCTION	19381940
QUANTITY	Saloon 1,577, Coupé 281
PRICE	Saloon £395, Coupé £415

SS JAGUAR 3½ LITRE SALOON AND DROPHEAD COUPÉ

MODELS	Four-door Saloon, Two-door Convertible (all-steel)
ENGINE	Overhead-valve 6-cylinder, 3485cc
MAX. POWER	125bhp
MAX. SPEED	91.8mph
PERFORMANCE	0-60 in 9 seconds
WEIGHT	Not available
LENGTH	Not available
WIDTH	Not available
IN PRODUCTION	1938-1940
QUANTITY	Saloon 1,065, Coupé 239
PRICE	Saloon £445, Coupé £465

JAGUAR MARK V 2½ LITRE SALOON AND DROPHEAD COUPÉ

MODELS	Four-door Saloon, Two-door Convertible
ENGINE	Overhead-valve 6-cylinder, 2663cc
MAX. POWER	102bhp
MAX. SPEED	87mph
PERFORMANCE	0-60 in 17 seconds
WEIGHT	32½cwt
LENGTH	15ft 7in
WIDTH	5ft 9in
IN PRODUCTION	1949-1950
QUANTITY	Saloon 1,647, Coupé 28
PRICE	Saloon £1,189 (1949) Coupé £1,247 (1950)

JAGUAR MARK V 3½ LITRE SALOON AND DROPHEAD COUPÉ

MODELS	Four-door Saloon, Two-door Convertible
ENGINE	Overhead-valve 6-cylinder, 3485cc
MAX. POWER	125bhp
MAX. Speed	92mph
PERFORMANCE	0-60 in 14.7 seconds
WEIGHT	32½cwt
LENGTH	15ft 7in
WIDTH	5ft 9in
IN PRODUCTION	1949-1951
QUANTITY	Saloon 7,814, Coupé 977
PRICE	Saloon £1,263, Coupé not available

models had changed very little from their pre-war specifications, except for modifications such as better brakes, new shock absorbers, and the standard fitting of a basic air-conditioning unit (intended for early 1940s models) that supplied heat to the car's interior and also functioned as a windscreen demister. Possibly as a result of the introduction of left-hand drive models, an inordinate number of these vehicles were destined to accompany American servicemen returning home after the war. Retrospectively, these models were classified Mark IV to distinguish them from those that would be introduced in 1949.

Jaguar launched their evolutionary post-war design the Mark V at the London Motor Show of 1948. By virtue of the fact that its bodywork was developed from the Mark IV, the new saloon retained a traditional style albeit enhanced by features such as the long, sweeping rear mudguards. Available only with the 2½- and 3½-litre engines, as Standard was no longer producing the 1½, the Mark V had a specially strengthened box-frame chassis and was notable for being the first Jaguar production car to feature independent front suspension. Over 1,000 examples of a drophead coupé version were produced, the majority for export.

The Mark V was undeniably a car that offered style, performance and value for money. But essentially it was a transitional car with no future, remaining in production for only one year, and even at its launch at the 1948 Motor Show it was overshadowed by Lyons' radical design for the 1950s: the XK series.

BELOW Mark Vs await their turn to be loaded onto the *Mauretania*. The steel quota system introduced after the war was intended to encourage exports, and scenes such as this became commonplace in the late 1940s and early 1950s.

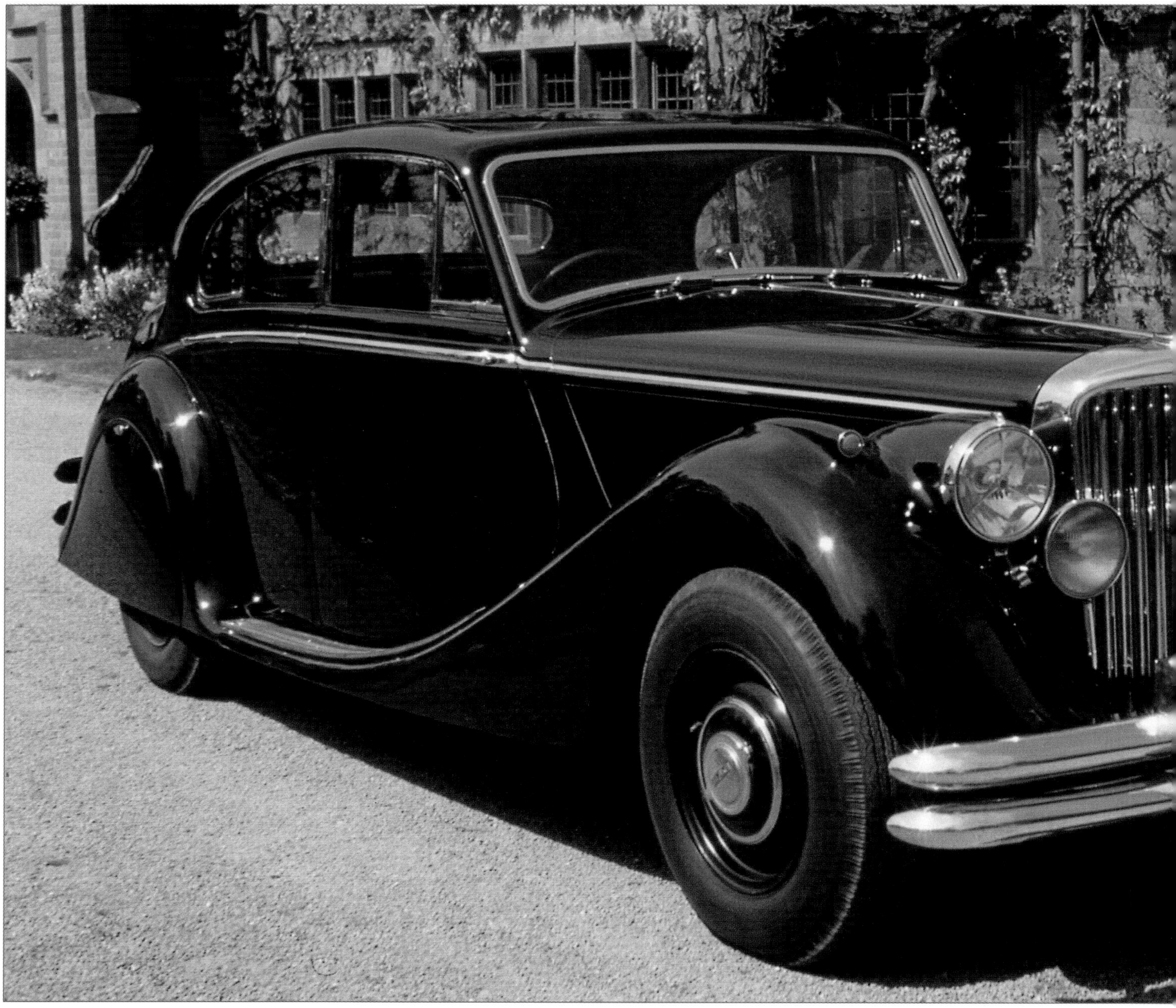

LEFT The car without a future. Times were difficult after the war, and Jaguar was unable to produce a completely new model, so the Mark V was launched to serve as an interim model prior to the introduction of the XK range. Available with only 2½ and 3½ litre engines, the Mark V retained the traditional design of its forbears and, at £1,263, was excellent value for money.

LEFT An example of the Mk V Coup de Ville.

The excellent 6-cylinder overhead-valve engine of the Mark V.

Chapter Three

Revolutionary Power

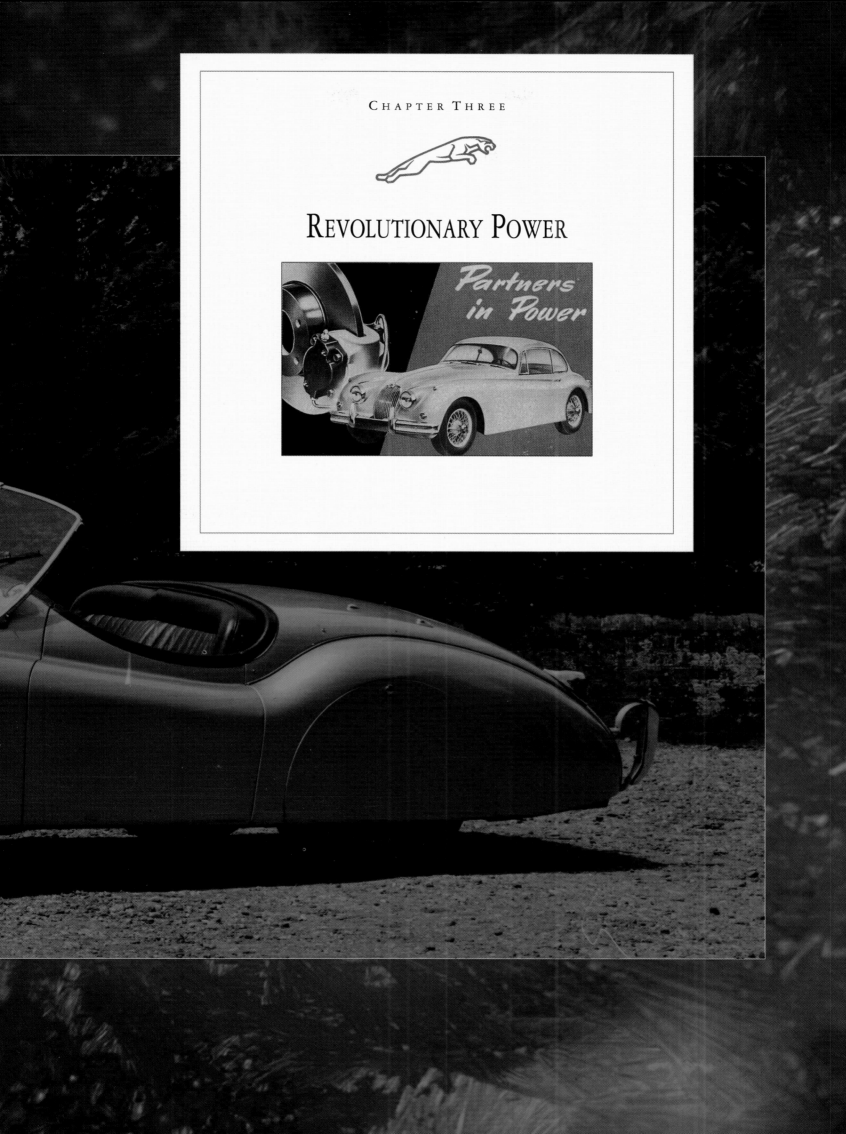

Six years of war had left Great Britain close to bankruptcy, and the government was keen for industry to export its products to countries such as the United States. American servicemen, familiar with the more utilitarian interiors of their country's automobiles, whilst posted in Britain and on the continent had discovered such suave interior features as walnut dashboards and leather upholstery, and were keen to impress their own countrymen with the quality and style of European models. Many of the more desirable sports cars were being transported home with their new owners, reflected in the fact that 35 per cent of Jaguar's total production was being exported in the years following the war.

But even with Weslake's overhead valves the former Standard engines were now approaching obsolescence, and Jaguar fully realized that if it wanted to compete with the more advanced automotive concepts now emerging from other European motor manufacturers, then it had to produce its own high-performance engine. During their fire-watching stints during the war, Lyons and his colleagues had spent many hours discussing advanced specifications and better performance for the post-war vehicles, and plans for a new engine were well in hand.

After the war the Jaguar engineers continued work on developing a modern six-cylinder 2½-litre engine capable of 160bhp; this engine size was chosen in consideration of post-war petrol rationing and because there was the possibility of taxation against larger engines. A smaller four-cylinder 1½-litre engine was also considered, which would share the dimensions and many components with the larger engine, thus enabling both units to be produced by the same machinery.

Beginning with XA (the X representing experimental), each design was allocated initials. The first to be built was in fact the sixth version, the four-cylinder 1360cc XF with hemispherical combustion chambers and, more significantly, twin overhead camshafts. Jaguar engineers were well versed in the advantage of this layout in that it produced more power, but were concerned about its drawbacks: the engines could be noisy because of

LEFT The XK120 was exceedingly popular in the United States, and most of the early models were exported across the Atlantic.

ABOVE Launched at the London Motor Show of 1948, the XK120 was initially limited to a production run of only 200 models. With the adoption of pressed-steel bodywork, however, over 2,500 of the Fixed Head version were produced.

the long trains of gears necessary to drive the camshafts, they were costly to make, had a tendency toward unreliability, and were awkward to service. Lyons, however, insisted on a 'twin cam' and his engineers worked on to produce further prototypes. The XG, with a single side camshaft and utilizing the Standard 1776cc engine, was found to be noisy and was supplanted by the 2-litre XJ with twin overhead cams, which in turn was developed into a six-cylinder 3182cc version. To compensate for the lack of torque, further modifications led to the final specification: the 3442cc XK.

The new XK engine was initially destined to power the new saloons that were to be launched in 1951. At the end of the 1940s, however, and with SS100 production having ceased during the war, Jaguar found itself in the position of having no sports car to embellish its range. Not wanting to delay introduction of the new XK engine for three years, Lyons expeditiously produced a sports car design based on a shortened form of the Mark V chassis and including the new engine: the result was the XK120.

When the XK120 was unveiled at the London Motor Show in 1948 an instant classic was born: here was the ultimate sports car that had everything. Bearing in mind the fact that the country was still stumbling

Rallye Des Alpes

The Rallye des Alpes was regarded in the 1950s as the toughest driving test of all, comprising three days and one night of concentrated motoring over some of the highest and most difficult mountain passes in Europe. Drivers and co-drivers had to carry out their own repairs, and were not allowed to change most parts on their cars should anything go wrong during the race. Driving conditions were hazardous in the extreme, with passes such as the Gavia having a loose surface and a one-thousand-foot unprotected drop on one side. Only a few passes were actually closed to the public during the race, however, and maximum speed trials were held on the open road, often with the local population joining in.

Originally known as the XK120 Super Sports, the Roadster was a fast and stylish car. NUB 120 became one of the most successful examples, taking Ian Appleyard to three successive Alpine Rally victories in the early 1950s.

back from the grim conditions of World War II, its population hungry for any kind of material excitement denied them during the war years, it is small wonder that the 120 was received to sensational acclaim. Justifiably, Lyons could accept the general opinion that his design was a work of art, and without doubt it was intended for speed. The engine – the world's first mass-produced unit with hemispherical combustion chambers and twin overhead camshafts – featured technical sophistication previously found only in the expensive world of racing cars: producing 160bhp, it was capable of powering the car to over 120mph, a fact that elevated the model to the status of fastest production car in the world. Yet with all this power, a durable chassis of immense strength and sumptuous bodywork, the XK120 was available at the unbelievable price of £1,263.

The first XK120, originally called the XK120 Super Sports but later known as the XK120 Roadster (an American term coined perhaps in view of the model's export potential to the United States), was built on an

ABOVE Stirling Moss and colleagues reminisce beside the car in which they travelled over 16,000 miles (the equivalent of two years' mileage) during one week in 1952.

aluminium body but over a traditional ash frame, as it was never intended that these cars would be mass-produced. Indeed, they were envisaged principally as a testing ground for the new 3442cc engine as well as an advertisement for the projected Mark VII that would use the same engine.

The initial production run was planned to output only 200 cars, but even during the course of the Motor Show it was realized that this number would be wholly inadequate. To satisfy demand, Jaguar consequently decided to adopt pressed-steel bodywork in place of the original aluminium coachwork, a decision that would delay production of the XK120 in larger numbers until the beginning of the 1950s.

Naturally enough, the promised performance trumpeted for the XK120 was lampooned in certain quarters of the press, and Lyons made preparations for an event at which he intended to silence his detractors. Thus, in May 1949 he arranged for a party of journalists to travel to the Jabbeke motorway in Belgium to witness speed trials. With consummate pride the test driver demonstrated that the XK120 could indeed fulfil its promise when it reached 126mph and, later, 132.6mph. At the time, speeds of this order could only be expected from a Ferrari V12 costing many thousands of pounds. Suitably humbled, the world's motoring press proceeded to laud the virtues of the car it had so readily deprecated.

Four months later XK120s were entered in the Production Car Race at Silverstone, a significant event in that it was the first big production-car racing event since the war. William Lyons was keen to show the world just how the XK120 could perform, and he provided virtually unmodified 120s for three of the country's finest drivers, Leslie Johnson, Peter Walker and

Prince Bira. In the event, the team would have taken first, second and third places had not a puncture prevented Bira from completing the course.

With the introduction of pressed-steel bodywork, production was realistically catching up with demand for the first time, and by 1951 almost all production cars were being shipped to the United States, many of them gracing the driveways of American film stars. In March of that year Jaguar introduced the Fixed Head Coupé. With a curvaceous steel roof that closely resembled that of the Mark VII, the Coupé incorporated such 'civilized' features as doors with exterior handles and manually operated windows, while the interior recalled the opulence of the pre-war saloon and was upholstered more luxuriously than the Roadster. A heater was fitted as standard, and for those who complained of too much interior heat in hot climates, front and rear quarter-lights had been added. Wire wheels, used increasingly on the competition 120s, were available as an option. All models of the Fixed Head Coupé were exported until 1953, when the first right-hand drive versions were produced. Surprisingly, less than 200 were manufactured with this arrangement and examples of the model are rarely found today.

Continuing his policy of lending cars to talented drivers for the primary purpose of publicity, in 1950 Lyons had supplied six near-standard aluminium XK120s to drivers Leslie Johnson, Peter Walker, Ian Appleyard, Clement Biondetti, Tommy Wisdom and Nick Haines. Johnson took his car to Mille Miglia where he finished fifth, then went on to take part in the Le Mans 24-hour race, attaining third place before brake failure led to an overstrained clutch and retirement from the race after 21 hours. Brake failure on similar cars was a common problem during this period due to the nature of the streamlined bodywork and was not satisfactorily overcome until the advent of disc brakes, a field in which Jaguar was to undertake much pioneering work, introducing them to production models over the next five years.

Two other XK120s took part at Le Mans in 1950, finishing in 12th and 15th places. Motoring enthusiasts were impressed by the performance of

TOP LEFT AThe XK140 was available with a wide range of colour schemes that were carefully co-ordinated for bodywork, interior and top.

ABOVE Replacing the XK120, the revolutionary XK140 was offered in Drophead, Fixed Head and Roadster form. A Drophead illustrates the prominent and robust bumpers that were incorporated in answer to requests by American customers.

Johnson's 120, particularly as the car differed little from the model that was widely available for purchase. Equally impressed was William Lyons, who appreciated the fact that racing success not only attracted free publicity but also promised potential commercial benefits, and he swiftly authorized the development of a more specialized version of the XK120: a dedicated competition sports car that would be able to take on the new Ferraris from Italy. This sports car was the C-Type – 'C' for competition – that would triumph at Le Mans in 1951.

Ian Appleyard, who had already enjoyed rally success in an SS100, won the 3-litre class event at the Alpine Rally, and was to repeat this achievement in 1951 and 1952. Appleyard had special connections with Jaguar, for not only was he an authorized dealer but was married to Pat, one of Lyons' daughters. The Appleyards were to become one of the world's most successful Jaguar competition teams in their XK120, registration NUB 120.

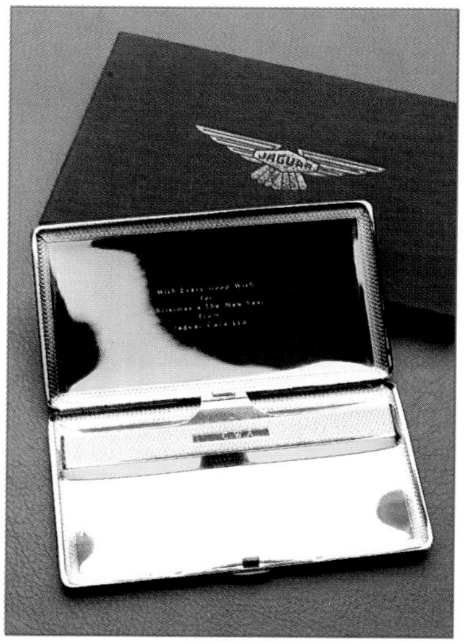

ABOVE A Jaguar cigarette case was only one of a number of enchanting little extras that were introduced during the 1950s.

BELOW The XK140 Roadster epitomized every Englishman's dream of what a Tourer should be, but in fact only 47 were destined for the British market while over 3,000 left-hand drive models were produced.

In August 1950 Peter Walker took first place in a one-hour race at Silverstone, and later in the year Phil Hill – later to be world champion – gained first place in the Pebble Beach Cup Race in California. Hill also won numerous other events, having bored-out his 120's cylinder block to 3.8 litres, an engine capacity that was to have great significance in Jaguar history.

Tommy Wisdom was offered a drive in a Jowett Jupiter for the 1950 Tourist Trophy held on Ulster's Dundrod circuit, and so lent his borrowed XK120 to a young Stirling Moss. In atrocious conditions Moss overtook Wisdom to win the classic TT race, and so impressed Lyons that he invited Moss to drive for Jaguar when the company ran a full works team of C-Types the following year. This was indeed an auspicious gesture for Moss whose 21st birthday was on the following day.

Other drivers who had successes with XK120s include Belgians Johnny Claes and Jacques Ickx, whose son later gained fame as a Grand Prix driver. The later XKs were not as successful in racing as the 120s, mainly because racing cars were rapidly becoming more sophisticated, and the future of Jaguar racing lay with the new C and D Types.

Competition triumphs continued in 1951 with Claes recording a victory at the Liège-Rome-Liège Rally, Appleyard winning the Tulip, Morecambe, and RAC Rallies as well as the Alpine Rally. Of notable importance were XKs taking first three positions both in the French Rallye Soleil, and at Silverstone where the young Stirling Moss headed the field.

In what may be considered a publicity stunt, an extraordinary event in motoring history was scheduled for the afternoon of 5 August 1952, the beginning of a trial during which an XK would travel over 16,000 miles in one week. For seven days and seven nights the 120 (in fact Bill Heynes's own Fixed Head Coupé) circled the track at Montlhery near Paris at over

XK120 Open Two-Seater Super Sports

MODEL	Open Roadster with hood
ENGINE	XK Twin overhead cam, 6-cylinder, 3442cc
MAX. POWER	160bhp
MAX. SPEED	120mph
PERFORMANCE	0-60 in 10 seconds
WEIGHT	25½cwt
LENGTH	14ft 6in
WIDTH	5ft 1½in
IN PRODUCTION	1949-1954
QUANTITY	1,175 (rhd), 6,437 (lhd)
PRICE	£1,263

XK120 Fixed Head Coupé

MODEL	Closed Two-Seater Coupé
ENGINE	XK Twin overhead cam, 6-cylinder, 3442cc
MAX. POWER	160bhp
MAX. SPEED	120mph
PERFORMANCE	0-60 in 9.9 seconds
WEIGHT	27½cwt
LENGTH	14FT 5IN
WIDTH	5ft 1½in
IN PRODUCTION	1951-1954
QUANTITY	195 (rhd), 2,484 (lhd)
PRICE	£1,775

XK120 Drophead Coupé

MODEL	Two-Seater Convertible with folding hood
ENGINE	XK Twin overhead cam, 6-cylinder, 3442cc
MAX. POWER	190bhp
MAX. SPEED	120mph
PERFORMANCE	0-60 in 9.5 seconds
WEIGHT	27½cwt
LENGTH	14ft 5in
WIDTH	5ft 1½in
IN PRODUCTION	1951-1954
QUANTITY	294 (rhd), 1,471 (lhd)
PRICE	£1,660

XK140 Drophead Coupé

MODEL	2+2 Convertible with folding hood
ENGINE	XK Twin overhead cam, 6-cylinder, 3442cc
MAX. POWER	190bhp
MAX. SPEED	129.2mph
PERFORMANCE	0-60 in 11 seconds
WEIGHT	28½cwt
LENGTH	14ft 8in
WIDTH	5ft 4½in
IN PRODUCTION	1954-1957
QUANTITY	479 (rhd), 2,310 (lhd)
PRICE	£1,664

XK140 Fixed Head Coupé

MODEL	Closed 2+2-Seater Coupé
ENGINE	XK Twin overhead cam, 6-cylinder, 3442cc
MAX. POWER	190bhp
MAX. SPEED	129.2mph
PERFORMANCE	0-60 in 11 seconds
WEIGHT	28cwt
LENGTH	14ft 8in
WIDTH	5ft 4½in
IN PRODUCTION	1954-1957
QUANTITY	843 (rhd), 1,965 (lhd)
PRICE	£1,616

XK140 Open Roadster

MODEL	Open Two-Seater Roadster
ENGINE	XK Twin overhead cam, 6-cylinder, 3442cc
MAX. POWER	190bhp
MAX. SPEED	121mph (S.E.)
PERFORMANCE	0-60 in 8.4 seconds (S.E.)
WEIGHT	27cwt
LENGTH	14ft 8in
WIDTH	5ft 4½in
IN PRODUCTION	1954-1957
QUANTITY	73 (rhd), 3,281 (lhd)
PRICE	£1,598

XK150 Open Two-Seater

MODEL	Open Two-Seater Roadster
ENGINE	XK Twin overhead cam, 6-cylinder, 3442 and 3781CC
MAX. POWER	As XK150 FHC and DHC
MAX. SPEED	136mph (3442cc 'S')
PERFORMANCE	0-60 in 7.3 seconds (3442cc 'S')
WEIGHT	28½cwt
LENGTH	Not available
WIDTH	Not available
IN PRODUCTION	1958-1960 (3442cc S.E., 'S') 19591960 (3781cc and 'S')
QUANTITY	1,297 (3442cc and S.E.) 888 (3442cc 'S') 42 (3781cc and S.E.) 36 (3781cc 'S')
PRICE	£1,666 (3442cc) £2,065 (3442cc 'S' and 3781cc) £2176 (3781cc 'S')

XK150 Fixed Head Coupé and Drophead Coupé

MODELS	2+2 Closed Convertible
ENGINE	XK Twin overhead cam, 3442 and 3781cc
MAX. POWER	190bhp (3442cc), 210bhp (3442cc S.E.) 220bhp (3781cc), 250bhp (3442cc 'S') 265bhp (3781cc 'S')
MAX. SPEED	123.7mph (3442cc S.E.) 132mph (3442cc 'S') 136.3mph (3781cc 'S')
PERFORMANCE	0-60 in 8.5 seconds (3442cc S.E.), 7.8 seconds (3442cc 'S') 7.6 seconds (3781cc 'S')
WEIGHT	DHC 28½cwt, FHC 29cwt
LENGTH	14ft 9in
WIDTH	5ft 4½in
IN PRODUCTION	1957-1960 (DHC 3442cc and S.E.) 1957-1961 (FHC 3442cc and S.E.) 19591960 (DHC 3442cc 'S') 1959-1960 (DHC 3781cc and 'S') 1959-1961 (FHC 3442cc 'S') 1959-1961 (FHC 3781CC AND 'S')
QUANTITY	Fixed Head Coupé 3,445 (3442cc and S.E.), 199 (3442cc 'S') 656 (3781cc and S.E.), 150 (3781cc 'S') Drophead Coupé 1,903 (3442cc and S.E.), 104 (3442cc 'S') 586 (3781cc and S.E.), 89 (3781cc 'S')
PRICE	Fixed Head Coupé £1,763 (3442cc), £1,940 (3442cc S.E.) £2,065 (3442cc 'S' and 3781cc) £2,175 (3781cc 'S') Drophead Coupé £1,793 (3442cc), £1,940 (3442cc S.E.) £2,093 (3442cc 'S') £1,970 (3781cc) £2,204 (3781cc 'S')

Originally produced in Fixed Head and Drophead versions, the XK150 range included a Roadster in 1958. All versions of the 150 were popular even if their very design concept was becoming obsolescent after ten years of evolution.

100mph. In so doing, the day-and-night driving team of Leslie Johnson, Stirling Moss, Jack Fairman and Bert Hadley actually clocked up 16,851 miles, the equivalent of two year's average mileage. Whether or not a publicity stunt, the occasion justly received widespread coverage attesting the superb quality of Jaguar engineering.

With increasing demand for XK120s and the forthcoming Mark VII, the company realized that it had outgrown its premises once again and began a search for a larger site in the area. It was fortuitous that another motor manufacturer, Daimler, was vacating its premises comprising one million square feet at Browns Lane, Allesley, on the outskirts of Coventry. Jaguar duly moved its operations onto this site, which is still the company's home after almost 50 years.

Another model of the XK120 was launched in April 1953 in the form of the Drophead Coupé that retained the comfortable and stylish interior of the Fixed Head Coupé and featured a folding hood in place of the steel roof. In contrast to the Roadster, in which it was considered normal to travel with the hood removed whatever the weather, it was intended that the Drophead hood should be down only in good weather because draughts were a problem due to the angle of the flatter windscreen.

In 1954 the reign of the XK120 came to an end after an eventful six years that had seen the sale of 7,612 Roadsters, 2,679 Fixed Head Coupés and 1,765 Drophead Coupés, the majority of models having been for export sale. At this time Britain was slowly but steadily regaining her feet and rebuilding her bombed-out cities, the constraints of shortages and rationing were near an end, and money was beginning to flow again into Britain's exchequer. The frequent representation of the 1950s as 'The

NOTES ON THE JAGUAR XK TYPE ENGINE

By W. M. Heynes, M.I.Mech.E., M.S.A.E. Chief Engineer, Jaguar Cars Ltd

In this new range of Jaguar engines all compromise in design has been eliminated. Each engine can be truthfully stated to incorporate all the most advanced technical knowledge available today on naturally aspirated petrol engines. Tests carried out on the completed units have shown the wisdom of the decision taken by the Jaguar Company nearly nine years ago to develop an engine on these lines.

In addition to bench tests, totalling many thousands of hours, extensive road tests at home and abroad have been carried out, and it is significant that the 2 litre engine, loaned to Colonel Gardner when he broke the world speed record in the 2 litre class at 176 miles per hour, is a completely standard unit with the exception of modified pistons to give a higher compression ratio. Further proof of the high efficiency of the XK engine was provided on the 30th of May, 1949, when an entirely standard production 3½ litre model running on pump petrol obtained a speed of 132.6 mph under the official observation of the Royal Automobile Club of Belgium. This speed is the highest ever recorded by a standard production car.

From the following condensed resumé of the more important features of the Type XK engine, it will be seen that no reliance has been placed upon the use of new or untried inventions. Instead, a blend of known and proved detail designs of the highest efficiency has resulted in the creation of a production engine of unparalleled quality and performance.

The following are some of the more important points:

Hemispherical head of high strength aluminium alloy with large diameter valves set 70°; the sparking plugs are disposed on the engine centre line in the path of the incoming gases. This ensures complete and rapid burning of the mixture, and ensures regular firing at slow speed pulling or maximum rpm.

VALVE SEATINGS:
These are of special high expansion cast-iron in which the coefficient of expansion approximates to that of the alloy cylinder head. This construction ensures a rapid flow of heat from the valve seat, eliminating local over-heating and giving an exceptional life to both valves and seatings.

INDUCTION SYSTEM:
The valve ports and induction system have been designed in collaboration with Mr Harry Weslake (generally accepted as the foremost expert in this science) and combine large induction passages, which offer a minimum restriction to flow, with specially contoured ports which ensure a controlled degree of turbulence in the combustion chamber.

TWIN OVERHEAD CAMSHAFTS:
Twin overhead camshafts, driven by two-stage chains, act directly on the valves through floating tappets. This reduces to a minimum the unsprung weight of the valve parts and enables extremely light valve springs to operate satisfactorily up to the high maximum rpm. In addition, the absence of rockers and push rods eliminate the main source of wear and noise often associated with overhead valve mechanisms. The camshaft and tappet face are submerged in an oil bath formed in the cylinder head casting, which forms an oil cushion between the two working surfaces.

OILING SYSTEM:
Large capacity oil pump is driven by skew gears on the front of the crankshaft and picks up oil from the sump through a floating strainer, which avoids cavitation, whilst the strainer ensures that no particles of dirt can enter the oiling system. On the delivery side of the pump all the oil is passed through a full-flow pressure filter and from there into a ½" diameter gallery, which runs the full length of the engine and from which distribution throughout the engine is taken.

COOLING SYSTEM:
Water circulation is supplied by high pressure centrifugal pump on the input side of the engine. This avoids any chance of steam pocketing, which can occur when the pump is used as an extractor. The water is fed from the pump down a separate gallery on the nearside of the cylinder block, and jets are directed on to the exhaust valve seatings and so across the head, around the sparking plugs, past the inlet valves, and passing out to the radiator through a gallery cast integral with the induction pipe. The block is cooled by a restricted circulation which gives a quick warm-up and maintains an efficient operating temperature under running conditions. The radiator block is of a film interspace type and is fitted with a thermostat control with a by-pass which controls the engine temperature.

CRANKSHAFT:
High tensile alloy steel forging with balance weights forged integral with the webs. The seven main bearings on the six-cylinder engines and the three main bearings on the four-cylinder engines are of 2½" diameter. The exceptionally large diameter of these bearings and the resulting crank rigidity are responsible to a large degree for the extreme smoothness with which these engines deliver their power, even up to the high maximum rpm of which they are capable.

BEARINGS:
The bearings are the Vandervell thin steel shell white metal lined type for crankshaft, connecting rods and camshaft bearings, and although these are precision made and completely interchangeable without fitting, they have proved to give practically unlimited life under more exacting test conditions.

PISTONS:
High strength aluminium alloy fitted with two narrow compression rings, the top ring being chromium plated to eliminate corrosion and consequent wear and, in addition, a slotted oil control ring is also fitted.

CONNECTING RODS:
Steel "H" section forging drilled up the centre web to provide oil feed to small end. The big end and cap are well ribbed to give rigidity and maintain true circular form under working stresses.

Ian Appleyard – A Rare Breed

Ian Appleyard was born in North Yorkshire in 1923. He gained a first-class engineering degree from London University and subsequently joined the Royal Electrical and Mechanical Engineers, attaining the rank of major at the age of 21. Following his military service he took over and expanded his father's motor dealership, Appleyards of Leeds, becoming a prominent businessman in the city until his retirement in 1988.

In what Appleyard described as "the Golden Age of Rallying", he achieved many notable rally triumphs with his wife Pat, whom he married in 1950. In the same year, William Lyons lent six XK120s to established drivers, including Appleyard, and the gleaming white car, registration NUB 120, was to become one of the most successful and well-known Jaguars. Appleyard entered and won the Alpine Rally in 1950, 1951 and 1952, achieving a Gold Coupe des Alpes for three successive penalty-free runs something the organizers had considered impossible, and a feat matched by only one other driver, Stirling Moss. The husband and wife team also won both the Tulip Rally and the International RAC Rally in 1951, as well as numerous other races worldwide, clocking up more than 100,000 miles in the process. NUB 120 is preserved in full running order by the Jaguar Daimler Heritage Trust.

For the European Rally in 1953 Appleyard swapped NUB 120 for a Mark VII, having been requested to do so "as an English Gentleman", for he was considered invincible in the XK120; even so, he came second. Appleyard attributed his continuing success to painstaking preparation. He would practise changing wheels and adjusting brakes, and would plan how to deal with any conceivable technical problem. Ian Appleyard's marriage to Pat was dissolved, and in 1959 he married Philippa ("Pip") Ryder.

When Appleyard retired he returned to a childhood interest, ornithology, and became well regarded for his work detailing rare breeds of bird in the Yorkshire Dales, particularly the ring ouzel. In 1994 he published Ring Ouzels of the Yorkshire Dales that was illustrated by his own photographs.

Ian Appleyard died in June 1998 at the age of 74.

Golden Age' was probably just as true at this time for industry eager to sell its products, as it was for domestic consumers eager to buy them.

The influence of export markets and racing engines had a direct bearing on Jaguar's next model, which was unveiled at the Earls Court Motor Show in October 1954. Incorporating suggestions from overseas dealers and mindful of the many modifications already undertaken on the XK120, Jaguar produced the XK140 which used the same pressed-steel bodywork as its forerunner and similarly was available in roadster, fixed head and drophead models.

Although sharing the same pressings as the 120, there were notable external differences including bumpers that were prominent and robust, and a radiator grille with thicker horizontal bars (in response to requests from American customers for something a little sturdier in time of need). Other transatlantic tastes were manifested by the appearance of a thin chrome strip on the bonnet and bootlid, and by the placing of the rear numberplate on a separate panel.

On the Roadster and Drophead models the bulkhead was moved forward by three inches to allow for more legroom a modification that also improved weight distribution and handling and for the provision of two small rear seats. The latter feature was designed to make these models more attractive to families with young children.

The Special-Equipment 3442cc XK engine was fitted as standard, and with a top speed of about 130mph the XK140 overtook the 120 as fastest production car in the world. Rack and pinion steering was incorporated, whilst optional overdrive was soon followed by the availability of automatic transmission, a feature dear to the hearts of customers in the United States.

A more powerful version of the XK140 was announced in 1955. Known as the XK140MC and powered by a 210bhp C-Type engine, this model was capable of 0-60 in eight seconds and boasted a top speed of 150mph. The designation was unofficial, however, as was that of the XK140M in the United States (the 'M' for modified engine). The upward trend in exports continued, a fact reflected, of course, in the relatively small number of right-hand drive models manufactured. Between 1954 and 1957, for example, only 73 out of a total of 3,354 Roadsters produced were right-hand drive models. Similar figures for the 2,808 Fixed Heads and 2,789 Dropheads were 843 and 479 right-hand drive models respectively.

In the last few months of 1956, the year in which William Lyons received a knighthood, Jaguar began a tentative programme of building production versions of the racing D-Types. Finding itself in the unaccustomed position of having more bodyshells than it could sell, the company decided to convert the remainder into road cars, a move that would benefit customers who wished to participate in competitions. By February 1957 less than 20 examples of the XKSS had been completed, however, before fire swept through the premises in Browns Lane, destroying the production line and much of the vital engineering equipment. That the company overcame this crisis was due in no small measure to the efforts of the workforce and, astoundingly, work resumed within two days. Although the 250bhp XKSS was essentially a 'civilized' version of the racing D-Type it bore a striking resemblance to the E-Type, and also matched its top speed of 150mph.

The XK150, viewed here in Drophead form, was designed mainly for the American market, and transatlantic tastes were catered for by the fitting of wrap-round bumpers and a one-piece windscreen.

Just four months after the Browns Lane fire the XK form was revised for the last time with the debut of the bigger and heavier XK150, designed very much with the American market in mind. With the chassis and body construction inherently the same as that for the XK140, the bodywork exhibited a noticeable trend toward modernism: the two-piece windscreen had given way to a singular one with strengthened glass, a slightly raised waistline and bulbous doors that had allowed interior space to be widened by four inches, a much wider radiator grille, and conspicuously stronger wrap-round bumpers.

If such exterior modifications were not to everyone's taste, the XK150 offered all-round superior performance. Special-Equipment models were fitted with the B-type cylinder head that developed only 190bhp but afforded a lot more torque in the middle range of performance. The lessons learnt from braking problems in competitive racing were applied to the production sports car market for the first time in the XK150's all-round powered disc brakes.

Resources were stretched in the months following the factory fire and Jaguar was able to produce only fixed head and drophead models in 1957, although a Roadster complemented the range during the following year. Also in 1958 the Weslake wizardry was evident in another addition to the marque, the XK150S that was powered by the same engine but featured triple SU carburettors and an optional straight port cylinder-head of Weslake's design. In this form the engine developed 250bhp, and 0-60 was achievable in under eight seconds. A year later, and continuing the upward power trend, Jaguar dropped an XC 3.8-litre unit into a 150S with the option of either the B-type or the 'S' straight-port cylinder head; engines with the 'S' head yielded an impressive 265bhp and endowed the 150XK with a top speed of 136mph and performance of 0-60 in 7.6 seconds.

Dating back to the late 1940s, the design philosophy of the XK series was now appearing somewhat outmoded, and after a steady succession of models, modifications and improvements Jaguar needed a sharp, eye-catching and radical design fitting for the dawn of the 'Swinging Sixties'.

TOP LEFT A sad sight at Browns Lane after fire had ripped through the workshops, destroying vital engineering equipment and all completed examples of the forthcoming XKSS. With true British grit and determination, though, employees and management recommenced production after only two days.

ABOVE Lessons learnt from competitive racing were applied to production sports cars for the first time, and resulted in the fitting of all-round disc brakes in the XK150s.

RIGHT The XK150's exterior design may have dated, but not to the detriment of interior comfort.

Chapter Four

The Golden Years

Even with the XK sports cars' continuing high level of popularity and the evolutionary Mark V's debut in 1949, a new look was needed for the dawn of the 1950s. It came in the large and voluptuous form of the Mark VII saloon that was unveiled at the Earls Court Motor Show of 1950. The result of many years' development and projected to sell in larger quantities than the XKs, its appearance was to assure Jaguar's continuing financial well-being for many years to come.

Its enthusiastic welcome in Britain was echoed later in the year when New Yorkers gained their first glimpse of the stunning new saloon, its sheer size and stylish upholstery appealing very much to American tastes. Servicemen returning after the war had already been impressed by the quality of the Jaguars they had driven whilst in Britain and were always in the market for large, sporty cars. Indeed, the Mark VII was designed specifically to appeal to the dollar market because steel rationing regulations still favoured those manufacturing companies that earned the most dollars.

Launched to the accompaniment of the Jaguar publicity department's now-famous epithet 'Grace, Space and Pace', the Mark VII was swiftly praised by the motoring press, the February 1952 edition of *Autocar* commenting after six months of road tests in England and Europe: '... in performance and in road behaviour, as in appearance and finish, this is one of the most impressive cars available in the world today'. The *Daily Mail* corroborated this testimonial with their opinion that the Mark VII was 'A world beater ... if ever there was one', and even *Sporting Life* was moved to comment on the 'sleek, streamlined six-seater with every luxury fitment possible'.

The chassis was the same as that used for the Mark V saloon, and the 3.4-litre XK120 engine had been moved forward by five inches to provide more legroom in the passenger compartment as well as increased bootspace, a feature particularly appealing to American buyers; rear-seat passengers also benefited from the adoption of full-width bodywork.

The wider bodywork was a cardinal asset to the handling of the Mark

LEFT The launch of the Mark VII in 1951 was accompanied by the company's famous epithet 'Grace, Space and Pace', and the high level of Jaguar opulence is illustrated in this interior view of a left-hand drive model.

ABOVE Considered large by British standards, the massive but modern form of the Mark VII was designed predominantly for the American market and represented yet another success for William Lyons. Rear-seat passengers benefited especially from the adoption of full-width bodywork.

VII, for despite its size and weight it was capable of 0-60 in under 14 seconds and a top speed of just over 100mph. In consideration of rocketing sales abroad and especially in the United States, automatic transmission became available on left-hand drive models in 1953, followed later by optional overdrive. During the three years it was in production almost 21,000 models were manufactured, and even though money had been devalued this sleek and streamlined 'world beater' was still a bargain at £1,276, including purchase tax – the Bentley Continental, one of its closest rivals, was over five times this amount.

With this particularly inspiring example of Lyons' designs, it is interesting to note his *modus operandi* of design technique (that was, remarkably, done by eye). He began events by verbally describing his ideas to a team of craftsmen who would build a mock-up of his vision in wood and metal, continuing with modifications until Lyons was satisfied. As in the case of the Mark VII, it was not until this point that draughtsmen actually prepared drawings of the tools needed to cast the body panels. Large panels took a great deal of time to prepare, and this fact explains one reason for the delay in the Mark VII's production.

Sales were further boosted early in 1952 when two Mark VIIs, driven by René Cotton and Jean Heurteaux, took fourth and fifth places in the Monte Carlo Rally, and Ian Appleyard came second in the Tulip Rally in April. A month later Stirling Moss drove a Mark VII to a convincing win in the Silverstone Production Touring Car Race, a victory that heralded Jaguar's domination of this event for the next 10 years. In 1953 Appleyard finished second place at Monte Carlo but took first in the Tulip Rally, while Stirling Moss repeated his triumph at Silverstone. Such results went on and on, and with the exception of Formula One racing it was almost guaranteed that Jaguar would be somewhere in the top five positions.

The Mark VIIM, an improved version of the Mark VII, appeared in September 1954. With the XK140's 190bhp engine and close-ratio four-speed gearbox, this was a much sportier car than its predecessor. Various styling changes were evident, including the replacement of the semaphore indicators by flashing signals. The Mark VIIM sold for £1,616, and 10,061 models were output during its three-year production life.

Through the introduction of the XKs and the Mark VII, Jaguar had deliberately concentrated on producing larger models in deference to export sales in the United States, and this course had left the Jaguar range without a smaller saloon more suitable for Europe's narrower roads. A car of this type would be cheaper to buy, insure and run, and could also attract American buyers who were looking for a smaller sporting car. To fill this gap in the market Jaguar had already considered a saloon powered by four cylinders rather than six, and an original XK100 engine underwent several tests and modifications but never achieved the required levels of smoothness

ABOVE Driven by Colin McMeekin, Dennis Bell and James Ross-Tomlin, a Mark VII takes up the Monte Carlo Challenge in 1960.

Mark VII Saloon

MODEL	Large Five/Six-Seater, Four-door Saloon
ENGINE	XK Twin overhead cam, 6-cylinder, 3442cc
MAX. POWER	160bhp
MAX. SPEED	101mph
PERFORMANCE	0-60 in 13.7 seconds
WEIGHT	34½cwt
LENGTH	16ft 4½in
WIDTH	6ft 1in
IN PRODUCTION	1951-1954
QUANTITY	12,755 (rhd), 8,184 (lhd)
PRICE	£1,276

Mark VIIM Saloon

MODEL	Large Five/Six-Seater, Four-door Saloon
ENGINE	XK Twin overhead cam, 6-cylinder, 3442cc
MAX. POWER	190bhp
MAX. SPEED	104.3mph
PERFORMANCE	0-60 in 14.1 seconds
WEIGHT	34½cwt
LENGTH	16ft 4½in
WIDTH	6ft 1in
IN PRODUCTION	1954-1957
QUANTITY	10,061
PRICE	£1,616

2.4 Saloon

MODEL	Compact Four-door Saloon
ENGINE	XK Twin overhead cam, 6-cylinder, 2483cc
MAX. POWER	112bhp
MAX. SPEED	101.5mph
PERFORMANCE	0-60 in 14.4 seconds
WEIGHT	Not available
LENGTH	Not available
WIDTH	Not available
IN PRODUCTION	1955-1959
QUANTITY	19,400
PRICE	£1,344

Mark VIII Saloon

MODEL	Large Five/Six-Seater, Four-door Saloon
ENGINE	XK Twin overhead cam, 6-cylinder, 3442cc
MAX. POWER	210bhp
MAX. SPEED	106.5mph
PERFORMANCE	0-60 in 11.6 seconds
WEIGHT	Not available
LENGTH	Not available
WIDTH	Not available
IN PRODUCTION	1956-1959
QUANTITY	6,212
PRICE	£1,830

3.4 Saloon

MODEL	Compact Four-door Saloon
ENGINE	XK Twin overhead cam, 6-cylinder, 3442cc
MAX. POWER	210bhp
MAX. SPEED	120mph
PERFORMANCE	0-60 in 9.1 seconds
WEIGHT	Not available
LENGTH	Not available
WIDTH	Not available
IN PRODUCTION	1957-1959
QUANTITY	17,340
PRICE	£1,672

Mark IX Saloon

MODEL	Large Five/Six-Seater Saloon
ENGINE	XK Twin overhead cam, 6-cylinder, 3781cc
MAX. POWER	220bhp
MAX. SPEED	114.3mph
PERFORMANCE	0-60 in 11.3 seconds
WEIGHT	34½cwt
LENGTH	16ft½in
WIDTH	6ft 1in
IN PRODUCTION	1958=1961
QUANTITY	10,009
PRICE	£1,995

Mark II Saloon

MODEL	Compact Four-door Saloon
ENGINE	XK Twin overhead cam, 6-cylinder, 2483, 3442 and 3781cc
MAX. POWER	120bhp (2.4), 210bhp (3.4) 220bhp (3.8)
MAX. SPEED	96.3mph (2.4), 120mph (3.4) 125mph (3.8)
PERFORMANCE	0-60 in 17.3 seconds (2.4) 12.7 seconds (3.4) 8.5 seconds (3.8)
WEIGHT	Not available
LENGTH	Not available
WIDTH	Not available
IN PRODUCTION	1959-1967
QUANTITY	25,070 (2.4), 28,660 (3.4) 30,070 (3.8)
PRICE	£1,534 (2.4), £1,669 (3.4) £1,779 (3.8)

Mark X Saloon

MODEL	Large Four-door Saloon
ENGINE	XK Twin overhead cam, 6-cylinder, 3781cc
MAX. POWER	265bhp
MAX. SPEED	120mph
PERFORMANCE	0-60 in 10.8 seconds
WEIGHT	37½cwt
LENGTH	16ft 10in
WIDTH	6ft 4in
IN PRODUCTION	1961-1964
QUANTITY	13,382
PRICE	£2,392

S-Type Saloon

MODEL	Medium-size Saloon
ENGINE	XK Twin overhead cam, 6-cylinder, 3442 and 3781cc
MAX. POWER	210 and 220bhp
MAX. SPEED	115 and 121mph
PERFORMANCE	0-60 in 13.9 and 10.2 seconds
WEIGHT	32 and 33cwt
LENGTH	15ft 7in
WIDTH	5ft 6½in
IN PRODUCTION	1964-1968
QUANTITY	9,830 and 15,070
PRICE	£1,669 and £1,758

Automatic Transmission and the Mark VII

Announced in 1950, the Mark VII was immediately popular on both sides of the Atlantic, its very size and traditional English interior styling appealing particularly to the American motoring public. Tastes and expectations were changing rapidly, however, and two or three years later most Americans buying a car of the Mark VII's quality wanted automatic transmission as a standard feature.

Companies such as Bentley and Rolls-Royce already incorporated this innovation, and Jaguar, not wanting to be left behind in the competitive international market, by 1954 had addressed the requirements of those customers more interested in labour-saving devices than sporting performance, and were offering an automatic gearbox as an optional extra to American buyers only.

The cost of developing their own automatic gearbox would have been prohibitive, so Jaguar adapted the American Borg-Warner box that was modified to suit the XK engine. The torque-convertor type transmission was similar to that used by Studebaker, but the shift lever was smaller and set in the dashboard. Also in 1954 Jaguar offered the option of overdrive in manual-gearbox cars, a fuel-saving feature that appealed to European drivers. A year later automatic gearboxes became available on right-hand drive models, and from 1956 most large saloons were fitted with automatic transmission.

and quietness. The company persevered, however, and eventually a 2.4-litre version of the 3.4 XK unit was revised until acceptable levels of noise and vibration had been achieved.

The resulting 2.4 Saloon was remarkable in that it had a body of unitary construction in place of the traditional separate body and chassis. Issigonis had used this technique of weight-saving construction for his Lightweight Special racing car before 1939, and the method had been investigated by Heynes and Hassan in their design work on jeeps during the war. Much of the development work on unitary construction was undertaken by Bob Knight, an engineer who was later to become Managing Director of the company. Knight experimented with various types of rubber to isolate the unit body and thus reduce vibration. The front sub-frame was mounted on rubber and supported the independent front suspension whilst the back axle was supported by trailing arms and cantilever springs; the result was a quiet, manoevrable car offering an exceedingly comfortable ride. Expected sales of the 2.4 in the United States didn't materialize, however, and the majority of the 19,000 saloons made between 1955 and 1959 ended up in the home market. It should be noted that, upon the introduction of the Mark II in 1959, the 2.4 Saloon became known as the Mark I.

The Mark VIIs continued to shine in competition racing. Ronnie Adams was just beaten to first place at Monte Carlo in 1954, but in the following year Appleyard, Adams and Vard were the proud recipients of the Charles Faroux Team Trophy. And success followed success in the Silverstone Production Touring Car Race when Appleyard, Rolt and Moss took first, second and third positions in 1954, the new factory team of Mike Hawthorn, Desmond Titterington and Jimmy Stewart (brother of Jackie) repeating this feat in 1955.

Three of the new 2.4 Saloons were entered for the race at Silverstone in 1956 but technical difficulties with two of the cars prevented a recurrence of the most recent triumphs, Duncan Hamilton taking only third place in the remaining car. Fortuitously, however, Jaguar had also entered two Mark VIIs in the race and Bueb saved the day by edging ahead to beat Ken Wharton's Austin Westminster into first place. It was a different story at Le Mans, however, when two Jaguars crashed within minutes of the start, leaving Bueb and Hawthorn to battle on in their car for the best part of 24 hours. Despite losing time with problems that required a number of pit stops, the pair struggled back from twentieth to finish in sixth place.

After the factory fire, the small band of engineers at Browns Lane was finding it increasingly difficult to cope with development work on new models whilst at the same time servicing the needs of the factory racing teams. As a result, the company declared that it was terminating its involvement in motor racing, although it continued to support private ventures.

October 1956 saw the appearance of the Mark VIII, an updated model of the Mark VII. Outwardly, and apart from the addition of Bill Rankin's Jaguar mascot on the bonnet as standard (hitherto this had been an optional extra), the car had changed little from its predecessor. A one-piece curved windscreen replaced the former split screen, and chrome strips were added along the sides to permit the application of an optional two-tone paint scheme; the radiator grille achieved more prominence within a deeper chrome surround, and the rear wheels were framed in cutaway spats to assist

ABOVE Sales of the Mark VII rocketed in the United States, and automatic transmission was offered on left-hand drive models in 1953.

BELOW A personalized numberplate gives a clue to this model's identity.

brake cooling. On the performance side the model benefited from a B-type cylinder head and twin exhausts, endowing the Mark VIII with a top speed of over 105mph. With the American market in mind, a small number of left-hand drive versions with power-assisted steering were built before the Mark VIII's short production run ended in April 1958.

In the last few months of 1956, British motorists (and particularly owners of thirsty cars) suffered directly from the Suez crisis and the resulting introduction of petrol rationing that allowed the purchase of only 10 gallons per month. If driven carefully a Mark VII could be coaxed into 23mpg, but even with such prudence its owner was limited to little over 200 miles of motoring a month, and owners of Mark VIIIs were even less fortunate. Jaguar did their bit to ease the displeasure by modifying the carburettors for improved consumption. Performance was affected, of course, but significant savings were achieved.

Not long after the factory fire at Brown's Lane Jaguar brought out the 3.4 Saloon, a more powerful version of the compact 2.4. Featuring twin exhausts and a B-type engine with twin SU carburettors, top speed leapt to a noteworthy 120mph and acceleration from zero to 60 took a fraction over nine seconds. A number of modifications were incorporated to support the larger engine, including stiffer suspension, more-robust engine mountings,

LEFT Replacing the Mark IX in 1961, the Mark X Saloon was of unitary construction and was significantly modernized over its predecessor. The interior featured a profusion of leather and walnut, and fold-out tables were a delightful and practical addition for rear-seat passengers.

ABOVE High-speed luxury could be enjoyed in the Mark X, and despite its weight the saloon was capable of cruising at over 100mph.

and a new rear axle with modified Panhard rod mounting. The extra heat generated by the bigger engine necessitated the fitting of a wider radiator grille, a modification that was also applied to the 2.4 Saloon soon afterwards. Jaguar produced 17,340 models during the production period 19571959, and the 3.4 (known as the Mark I from 1959) was remarkable value for money at £1,672.

Disc brakes were offered on both the 2.4 and 3.4 saloons from the beginning of 1958, and their advent was particularly reassuring to racing drivers. Brake failure had long been a common problem on racing cars due to the nature of the streamlined bodywork. Although streamlining contributes toward the attainment of higher speeds, the all-enveloping nature of the bodywork results in the lack of a sufficient supply of cooling air to drum brakes, which consequently suffer at these higher speeds. The problem was enhanced by the practice of reducing wheel sizes to

ABOVE The 420 was an interim model introduced in 1967 but production lasted only for one year before the emergence of the XJ6.

OPPOSITE Many 2.4 Saloons were exported to Canada, but despite great expectations, sales of the saloon were disappointing in the United States.

accommodate the new racing tyres and also by the fitting of smaller-diameter drum brakes inside these smaller wheels.

The final embodiment of a design introduced in 1950 but little changed during the intervening years appeared at the Earls Court Motor Show of 1958. The Mark IX was given an XK engine bored out to 3.8 litres and developing 220bhp, a favoured powerplant of the racing teams. The Mark IX was a heavy car and was endowed with power steering after its initial introduction, and the task of stopping it was entrusted to disc brakes that replaced the previous drums. Interior comfort was enhanced by leather upholstery and, in a gesture possibly aimed toward those with continental motoring in mind, the car included a sun roof and a complete set of hand tools.

Although the Jaguar factory had withdrawn from competition, private entrants continued to try their hand at fast road and circuit racing, for which the Tour de France was the ultimate testing ground. In the Touring class event, Sir Gawaine Baillie took third place in 1958, but da Silva Ramos won the following year in the first of a series of successes for Jaguar; and Tommy Sopwith, manager of Equipe Endeavour and also Baillie's team leader, won a number of circuit races in his 3.4 during 1957 and 1958.

In the first British Touring Car Championship in 1958, Sopwith and Baillie teamed up and achieved a number of wins, whilst Hamilton, Hansgen and Hawthorn recorded several triumphs in 3.4 saloons, although it would be one of Hawthorn's last victories before he was killed on the road just after having become world champion.

The Earls Court Motor Show of 1959 saw the launch of the Mark II, a compact replacement for the 2.4 and 3.4 Saloons and the last real sports saloon the company made. At first glance it was very similar to its predecessors, yet there were a number of refinements to catch the eye: a new radiator grille with a thicker centre bar flanked by spotlights in place of the earlier small circular grilles, sidelights atop the front wings, slimmer roof pillars, chrome side-window frames, and a large rear wrap-round rear window. There was also a surprise on the inside in that the dashboard was completely revised, the central cluster of instruments having given way to a layout wherein the main instruments were now positioned either side of the steering column, an arrangement that would become standard in Jaguar cars.

In an ostentatious moment at the New York Motor Show a year later, William Lyons bewildered visitors by displaying a Mark II with gold-plated trim inside and out, accompanied by a model who wore a gold-embroidered dress and an £18,000 tiara. Such indecorous extravagance was unbecoming from William Lyons, and he made no attempt to keep the car which was reportedly dismantled afterwards. In 1998, however, two Jaguar devotees in America, Robert and Paula Alexandra, decided it was time to relive these golden memories and set to work recreating the car down to the last detail.

The initial 2.4- and 3.4-litre Saloons were soon joined by a 3.8-litre model that was the brightest star of the range. With the six-cylinder 3781cc engine and a power output of 220bhp it was capable of truly scintillating performance. With overdrive a top speed of 125 or even 130mph was attainable, and in the early 1960s the Mark II was celebrated as the fastest saloon on the road. Part of the model's success was its excellent power-to-weight ratio, a fact not lost on British police forces who,

Empire Building

In keeping with the contemporary trend of 'empire building', William Lyons purchased a number of companies in his ongoing quest for self-sufficiency and perfection. Shortly before the war, he bought out Motor Panels Limited, one of his major body panel suppliers. However, the business failed to prosper, and Lyons, needing capital to return to vehicle production in 1945, sold the company on to Rubery Owen.

Another significant acquisition was that of the Daimler Company in 1960. Jaguar continued to produce Daimler buses and lorries as well as limousines and sports cars, although in time these vehicles were to become Daimler versions of Jaguar models.

In the early 1960s Guy Motors, famous for introducing four-wheel brakes, Britain's first six-wheeled double-deck bus, and the world's first six-wheeled double-deck electric trolleybus, was in financial difficulty. William Lyons bought the assets of the company and restored the profitable production of lorries and passenger vehicle chassis.

Jaguar acquired Coventry Climax in 1963, a company formed sixty years earlier and famous world-wide for its engines, and during the following year purchased Henry Meadows Ltd, an engineering company founded in 1919. This was his last acquisition before Jaguar itself merged with the British Motor Corporation, which itself became British Motor Holdings immediately after the merger.

ABOVE Another addition to the 'compact' range, the 3.4 Saloon was modified to accept the larger engine. The new model could be recognized instantly by its larger radiator grille with additional vertical slats.

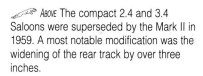

ABOVE The compact 2.4 and 3.4 Saloons were superseded by the Mark II in 1959. A most notable modification was the widening of the rear track by over three inches.

after a thorough testing programme of the Mark II in 1959, operated these small fast saloons in many parts of the country.

Of all the superlatives bestowed on the Mark II, versatility was certainly one worthy of consideration. By reason of speed and agility it found favour not only with the criminal fraternity but also with the very fast long arm of the law (interestingly, maximum speed limits were not imposed when Britain's first motorway opened in 1959, so an attempted escape with the Mark II at full throttle was not in itself against the law), whilst at the same

ABOVE On the Mark II sidelights appeared on top of the wings, spotlights replaced the former grilles, and a vertical bar was added to the radiator grille.

ABOVE Mark II models were available with 2.4, 3.4 and 3.8 versions of the magnificent XK twin-cam engine.

time maintaining distinct respectability as the conveyor of businessmen from the stockbroker belt. And naturally the 3.8 excelled in the field of competitive racing.

From 1960 rallies were increasingly changed to off-road courses, a milieu not suited to heavy Jaguar saloons, so the company switched its support to the Tour de France, a decision that immediately bore fruit when Bernard Consten and Jack Renel were to thrash all other contenders at the event for four years running. In circuit racing, 3.8s were driven to success in 1960 by

ABOVE A close-up of the Mk II 3.4 dashboard showing the automatic selector lever.

Roy Salvadori, Stirling Moss, Graham Hill and Jack Sears, whilst Lotus constructor Colin Chapman triumphed in a Coombs car at Silverstone before ordering a 3.8 for his personal use, and the medium became even more competitive in 1961 after the arrival of a 3.8 team comprising Dennis Taylor, Bruce McLaren and John Surtees.

If visitors to London's annual Motor Show were accustomed to a surprise or two from Jaguar, they were not disappointed when the Mark IX's successor was unveiled in 1961. Weighing-in at 35cwt, the massive Mark X was the first of a new generation of Jaguar saloons, and one of the widest cars ever made in Britain. Of unitary construction and designed specifically for the American market, the bulky Mark X had a wider version of the new independent rear suspension that assisted handling and offered a much

ABOVE Visually and mechanically enhanced over their predecessors, the Mark IIs were very fast and reliable and were to play an important part in securing Jaguar's future prosperity.

ABOVE Featuring a larger boot and new independent rear suspension, the much-acclaimed S-Type introduced in 1963 never really caught the imagination of the motoring public, and sales were consequently disappointing.

smoother ride to rear-seat passengers. Using the same 265bhp engine as the E-Type (also launched in 1961) and despite its weight, the saloon was exceedingly fast and was capable of cruising at an effortless 120mph.

The high hopes invested in the Mark X were not immediately fulfilled for two contiguous reasons. Although designed primarily for customers in the United States the very essence of the Mark X was somehow too conservative for American tastes, whilst in Britain its success was overshadowed by the continuing popularity of the compact Mark II, its very size being better suited to narrower British roads. This exposition is reflected in the fact that only 13,382 models of the Mark X appeared during its three-year production period. In an effort to rekindle interest Jaguar later released the Mark X with a 4.2-litre engine, but the venture was not successful with sales totalling only 5,137. Notwithstanding these setbacks, however, the Mark X represented the beginning of a concept that would evolve and spawn the superlative models of the 1970s and 1980s.

As the Mark X was being introduced Jaguar's production facilities were at bursting point, and the company bought out Daimler, Britain's oldest car manufacturer. As well as acquiring trucks, cars and limousines, Jaguar inherited two exceptional engines, the 4½- and 2½-litre Daimler V8s, and the latter soon replaced the XK unit in the 2.4-litre Mark II Saloon.

Whilst Jaguar was producing larger and larger saloons there was a growing demand for a more luxurious version of the compact saloon, and to assuage this requirement Lyons combined the most successful elements of both the Mark II and the Mark X to produce the S-type in 1963. Available with either 3.4- or 3.8-litre engines and benefiting from independent rear suspension and exterior restyling, the S-type was a splendid car that certainly filled a gap in the market, but its disappointing reception only resulted in sales around the 25,000 mark during its production life from 1964 to 1968.

CHAPTER FIVE

CATS ON TRACKS

JAGUAR
WINS LE MANS
FOR THE THIRD TIME IN FOUR YEARS

Following the impressive performance of three XK120s at Le Mans in 1950, William Lyons realized that a dedicated competition model would have an excellent chance of winning the race in 1951. Since its introduction in 1948 the XK120 had proved to be a fine production road car, but its heavy chassis and bodywork precluded it from racing, although the front suspension was ideally suited to such gruelling work and the engine would be ideal if it were modified to output more power. If the engineering team could overcome these shortcomings then Jaguar would be well on the way to sending a real winner – an XK120C, or C-Type – to Le Mans in 1951. The sports racing car project was thus inaugurated: Bob Knight would be responsible for project development, with Heynes undertaking the fundamental design of the C-Type and Malcolm Sayer providing drawings for the bodywork.

Although originally called the XK120C, the ultimate C-Type was almost unrecognizable from its forebear. The chassis comprised a frame of weight-saving welded tubes that endowed it with tremendous strength without forfeiting essential rigidity, and, to accompany the independent front suspension, the standard leaf-spring rear suspension was replaced by torsion-bar suspension with trailing links that afforded superior adhesion. The lighter rear suspension was found to be inferior on poor road surfaces, but this fact was irrelevant on the splendidly smooth track at Le Mans. A new high-pressure cylinder head and bigger carburettors together with an advanced exhaust increased the power of the XK engine to 210bhp.

The aluminium lightweight C-Type bodywork was made in three sections that were bolted to the frame, and the whole body was easily removable to facilitate access to the frame, engine and transmission, and suspension; additionally, the front end was hinged to reveal the engine housing. Rack and pinion steering replaced the 120's ball steering, and braking was provided by Lockheed self-adjusting drums.

At the time of Lyons' decision to proceed with the project, however, the Jaguar engineering department was engrossed in development work for the Mark VII Saloon, and had only six months in which to prepare the competition XK, a seemingly impossible task by any standards. Lyons had arranged for four lightweight XK120s to be prepared in case the C-Types were not ready for the 24-hour marathon, but his faithful development team worked hard to ensure that the three C-Types were completed in time. Three of the lightweight 120s were subsequently sold to an American dealer for racing on the west coast of the United States.

Le Mans provided the ideal stage for the C-Type's first appearance, and in 1951 the opposition comprised five Aston Martins, three 5.4-litre Cunninghams, 2½- and 4-litre Ferraris, a 3.8-litre Healey, and six Lago Talbots (the winners in 1950). With the teams of Moss/Fairman, Biondetti/Johnson and Walker/Whitehead leading the field after the first few laps it appeared that Lyons' dream would be fulfilled, but then disaster struck as Biondetti's car limped into the pits with the oil-pressure gauge reading zero. When the fault was identified as a fractured oil pipe, it was feared that the condition might also afflict the other two cars, a fear that was realized when Stirling Moss dropped out with the same problem. It was third time lucky, however, and Walker and Whitehead cruised home seven miles ahead of the nearest Talbot, and at a record speed of

Malcolm Sayer was the designer of the sleek bodywork for the C-Type, the company's first dedicated sports racing car. Intended specifically for competition at Le Mans, the model was capable of over 140mph, and eleven works cars were produced between 1951 and 1953.

93.49mph. Undeterred by the setback suffered at Le Mans, C-Types ventured onto the uneven surface of the Dundrod circuit where Stirling Moss won the 1951 Tourist Trophy, Walker and Rolt finishing in second and fourth places respectively.

Mindful of even greater victories to come, Jaguar completed eleven C-Type works cars between 1951 and 1953. These cars were managed by 'Lofty' England who, considering his own racing experience and extensive knowledge of the British racing scene, had wisely been promoted from Sales Manager to Jaguar Team Manager. As well as works cars, Jaguar also built 43 'production' C-Types, each one selling for £2,327. The production versions were specifically intended for club drivers, particularly those in the United States, who wanted to show their mettle against comparable Ferraris

Ecurie Ecosse

Ecurie Ecosse has a fascinating history from its origins in 1952, when it was set up by former driver David Murray and mechanic 'Wilkie' Wilkinson with the aim of creating a racing team to compete at circuits around the world.

Initially the team comprised three drivers, Ian Stewart, Bill Dobson and Sir James Scott-Douglas, all of them owning XK120s. Joining the all-Scottish racing team that was also established in 1952, they quickly amassed ten first, six second and six third places at club events. Ecurie equipped itself with three C-Types during the following year and took part in three European events before Jaguar offered the team disc-braked C-Types. Dobson had left the team by this time, and the squad was boosted by the arrival of Ninian Sanderson and Jimmy Stewart.

In 1954 Ecurie Ecosse won twelve of the seventeen events they had entered, and Jaguar was moved to sell the team three D-Types. Ecurie won seven out of twelve events in 1955, but it was at Le Mans in 1956 that the team stamped its name on motor racing. Against the works-supported thoroughbreds of the mighty giants such as Jaguar and Ferrari, Ecurie had the effrontery to enter a single D-Type driven by Ninian Sanderson and Ron Flockhart. In the event the three Jaguar works cars fell well before the finishing post, and the bold entry from the Scottish team surprised everyone by taking first place.

The Jaguar works team retired from racing in October 1956, a fact that spurred Ecurie to participate in the 1957 marathon in which it entered three D-Types and, in a tour de force for Scottish esteem, overcame a number of difficulties to finish in first and second places. Ecurie Ecosse continued to race successfully for a few more seasons before lowering the curtain on a decade of considerable achievement.

on the smaller circuits. These drivers enjoyed a moderate amount of success, but because the C-Types had been designed specifically for faster circuits such as Le Mans, they were never at their best on the poorer tracks of minor racing venues.

Alongside the debut of the C-Types, other Jaguar-engined cars built by independent enthusiasts began to appear in competition. One such sports car was built for Phil Scragg by engineer John Heath. Called the HW-Alta-Jaguar (the 'HW' referred to John Heath's garage), it featured a modified Alta Grand Prix chassis and a highly tuned XK engine, and was the vanguard in a series of HWM-Jaguars. Oscar Moore, a car distributor, equipped his Alta-engined HWM with a 3.8-litre Jaguar engine in 1952

and went on to spectacular success in British club racing during that year, and in 1955 British racing-car builders Cooper supplied a Jaguar-engined special for Walker to compete against the HWM-Jaguars, but the project was not as successful.

Throughout the year following the 1951 Le Mans race Jaguar continued improvements to the C-Type racers, and in association with Dunlop developed a new disc-braking system that proved to be very satisfactory in the 1952 Mille Miglia. Stirling Moss crashed during this road race, but left Italy with glowing impressions of the speed and performance of the Mercedes 300SLR. So insistent was he about the untapped potential of the Jaguar cars, moreover, that the company hurriedly streamlined their bodywork with a long drooping nose for higher maximum speed, and with a revised cooling system necessitated by the newly streamlined bodywork. There had been insufficient time for exhaustive testing before the all-important 24-hour race at Le Mans, however, and overheating forced all three cars out of the race. But with the Reims 12-hour race beckoning, Jaguar refitted the original bodies and the C-Types went on to win the event, later that year entering the Monaco Grand Prix in which Stirling Moss was involved in a multiple crash but Walker finished in sixth place.

At the same time as Jaguar were holding discussions with Dunlop over the acquisition of its disc brakes, millionaire Briggs Cunningham, of Cunningham roadster fame in America, had also been talking to Dunlop along similar lines. Cunningham automobiles had entered Le Mans three times without a win and their builder was convinced that these failures were due to inferior drum brakes rather than any lack of power from the Chrysler engines. The American thought his problems were solved when Dunlop elected to meet his requirements, but the company later reneged on the agreement because of their deal with Jaguar. Cunningham claimed that

ABOVE At the start of Le Mans in 1951, Whitehead and Walker race away ahead of two Cunninghams.

RIGHT Le Mans 1953: Rolt and Hamilton took the lead after fuel starvation had forced Stirling Moss's C-Type into the pits.

Dunlop had renounced the deal because the company might have lost a possible contract with Jaguar for disc brakes on production cars.

If Le Mans in 1952 was a calamity for the Jaguar stable, the 1953 race was to be one of memorable distinction. The introduction of a Manufacturers' Championship had tempted eighteen manufacturers (but without Mercedes this time) to compete alongside the world's foremost Grand Prix drivers, including world champions Ascari, Fangio and Farina. Onlookers may have been tempted into dismissing the Jaguar challenge prematurely when the C-Types lined up, enshrouded in their original bodywork. But the bodywork and chassis were now of lighter construction, however, and other significant modifications included new disc brakes, themselves improved since their initial and successful trial in the previous year's Mille Miglia, twin-choke Weber carburettors and stronger rear suspension.

Moss and Walker overtook the 4½-litre Ferrari of Villoresi and Hawthorn after only a few laps, and in customary manner Moss set a scorching pace for about an hour until his habitual bad luck struck again, and he stuttered into the pits with fuel starvation, a problem that occurred several times before it was finally solved. With Moss now trailing in twenty-first position, Rolt and Hamilton took the initiative and accelerated into first place, a position they held for the remainder of the race. Moss and Walker made up a tremendous amount of ground to finish in second place, while Whitehead and Stewart took fourth.

ABOVE Malcolm Sayer's experience of aircraft technology and aerodynamics was embodied in the stunning form of the D-Type.

ABOVE LEFT Rolt and Hamilton on their way to victory at Le Mans in 1953. Disc brakes contributed enormously to the C-Type's success.

XKSS

MODEL	Refined version of D-Type Two-Seater Sports Racing Car
ENGINE	XK Twin overhead cam, 6-cylinder, 3442cc
MAX. POWER	250bhp
MAX. SPEED	149mph
PERFORMANCE	0-60 in 5.2 seconds
WEIGHT	Not available
LENGTH	Not available
WIDTH	Not available
IN PRODUCTION	1957
QUANTITY	16
PRICE	£3,878

Interestingly, the winners had actually been 'disqualified' before the start of the race because of a minor infringement of practice regulations, but were reinstated after what must have been a fascinating tête-à-tête between William Lyons and the race organizers.

The overall result was a momentous triumph for Jaguar even though it was a 1-2-4. In cringing irony, third place was taken by a Cunningham, and the American must have pondered long and hard on what might have been if his deal with Dunlop had gone through. Significantly, perhaps, the C-Types were the only cars in the race fitted with disc brakes, and their importance was crucial to the Jaguar drivers in their ability to brake later for cornering and thus save vital seconds on each lap.

If the C-Type was seemingly at the apex of its mechanical potential, its bodywork was certainly capable of further refinement for higher speed, and to this end a development car, in fact a prototype of the D-Type, was produced in 1953. Later afforded the amorphous label 'C/D', this car had

The 3½ litres of raw but refined power under the bonnet endowed the D-Type with a top speed of over 160mph.

the unmistakable characteristics of the E-Type that would not appear for another seven years.

The design resulted in one of the most exquisite and remarkable racing sports cars of all time. It was aerodynamically superior to the C-Type and, as a result of techniques learnt through wartime work on aircraft, the centre section was a monocoque construction of magnesium alloy with double-skinned front and rear bulkheads, ahead of which a tubular sub-frame carried the engine and front suspension. As with the C-Type, the front end was hinged to allow access to the engine, suspension and wheels, and the rear bodywork was also removable.

The 3½-litre engine, mounted at an eight-degree angle and dry-sumped to reduce both the height of the engine and frontal area, was modified to output 250bhp, and adjustments were made to the inlet valves, camshafts and exhaust manifolding. The result was a power unit of phenomenal potential: zero to 60 in an unbelievable 4.7 seconds – almost twice as fast as

the C-Type – and a top speed of 162mph for 'production' cars and over 170mph for the sports racing version. Other improvements included a new gearbox, an improved disc-braking system, and light-alloy wheels that replaced the C-Type's wire wheels.

Expectations were high as three D-Types emerged for the 1954 Le Mans race against an awesome opposition of Alfa-Romeos, 4.9-litre Ferraris and the Mercedes 300SLR. In very wet conditions Moss, almost by tradition, was the pacemaker at an early stage until misfiring difficulties forced him into the pits, a number of other cars being similarly afflicted. Valuable time was lost through this exigency but, although Moss re-entered the race, brake troubles forced him to retire early. Some time later the Wharton/Whitehead D-Type lost its gears and dropped out. Only the Rolt/Hamilton car was left in the running, and in atrocious conditions Hamilton pounded forward in pursuit of the leading Ferrari at speeds often in excess of 170mph. At one point the Ferrari lost an additional seven minutes after refusing to start after a pit stop, enabling the D-Type to close the gap to just one and a half minutes. But after the rain stopped and the track began to dry out, the growling fury of the 4½-litre Ferrari surged Gonzales into the lead and to victory by two miles.

The Jaguars took a little sweet revenge on the Ferraris a month later, however, during the 12-hour event at Reims. In habitual fashion Moss set a blistering pace which the Ferraris couldn't match, but his premature

ABOVE The cockpit of a D-Type: the throne behind the power.

ABOVE LEFT The D-Type's engine was inclined at an 8-degree angle in order to reduce frontal area.

Le Mans 1955

The legendary Le Mans race is a fast and ferocious test of man and machine, and in 1955 was the scene of one of the most horrific crashes in motor racing history. During the early laps of the race Mike Hawthorn and his co-driver Ivor Bueb were racing neck and neck with Fangio's Mercedes and Castelotti's Ferrari, the lap record being broken ten times in the first two hours.

Pierre Levegh, driving for Mercedes, was battling it out with two other cars when, suddenly, he collided with an Austin-Healey and lost control in a catastrophe that also involved Hawthorn in his D-Type. The Mercedes disintegrated and caught fire as it lunged into the crowd, killing Levegh and 81 spectators, and injuring over a hundred more.

Amazingly the race continued, Bueb taking over from the stunned Mike Hawthorn, but the whole Mercedes team was later withdrawn. Months later Mercedes declared that it was retiring from motor racing, and more than thirty years elapsed before the company returned to the race track.

14

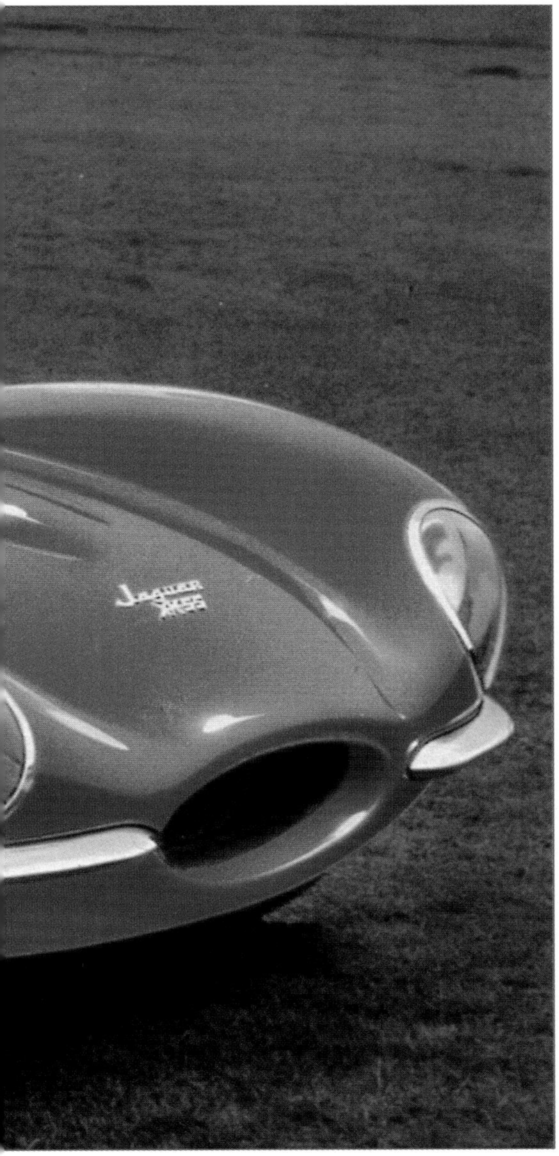

retirement allowed his team-mates to take first and second positions.

For 1955 the D-Types were further improved with longer-nosed bodywork, the bonnets having been lengthened by 7½ inches for better air penetration and to take full advantage of the car's aerodynamic qualities. Modifications were also effected to the engine, with power output increased to 275bhp. For racing on the shorter circuits, where maximum speeds were not attainable, some D-Types had their tailfins removed to save weight and drag.

Apart from mechanical revisions to the cars for the 1955 race, there had also been one or two changes of drivers, Stirling Moss having been enticed to the Mercedes stable, his place having been taken by Mike Hawthorn who had in turn been lured from Ferrari. The opening stages of the race were focused on Fangio's Mercedes, Hawthorn's D-Type and Castelotti's Ferrari as they raced neck and neck for two hours, during which time the lap record was broken no less than ten times. The frenetic pace proved too much for the Ferrari, which was forced to retire before the horrifying accident involving Levegh's Mercedes and Macklin's Austin-Healey. The entire Mercedes team was later withdrawn from the race, and with the Ferraris and two out of the three D-Type's having retired, it was a hollow victory indeed for Hawthorn.

In 1956 the 24-hour race was not a memorable one for Jaguar, with the Hawthorn/Bueb team struggling back from twentieth position to finish in sixth place, and in October the company announced their temporary retirement from racing. It was to be over thirty years, however, before Jaguar returned to the racetrack.

Between 1954 and 1956 the D-Types were built to a total of 71. Production versions sold for £3,878 and were raced by private club teams world-wide. The modern craze for collectibles encompasses a market for almost every conceivable item ever made, and this is no less true for the D-Type which, as one of the fastest and most beautiful racing cars ever made, is still one of the most coveted and desirable.

LEFT In the XKSS, Jaguar attempted to modify a D-Type as a production road car.

BELOW Under the appreciative eye of a gendarme, a D-Type roars to victory at Le Mans.

HDU 555N

Chapter Six

E for Excellence

Jaguar 4.2 XK-E Coupe, Roadster & 2+2 Family Coupe
"A different breed of cat"

Launched at the Geneva Motor Show in 1961, the E-Type was probably the most beautiful sports car of the decade. Its thrilling yet graceful contours were the result of the fertile and far-sighted imagination of Malcolm Sayer who applied the principles of aerodynamics to his bodywork designs. The E-Type was first available in Roadster (above) and Fixed Head Coupé forms.

After twelve years, the efficacy of the XK concept had become rather outmoded and many of its inceptive characteristics were now plainly outdated. Admittedly the engine was still a first-class unit (although many manufacturers in the United States were now fitting V8 engines) and performance had benefited greatly from the advent of disc brakes, but the chassis was becoming obsolescent, the bodywork was no longer in vogue, and the car itself was too heavy. Evidence of these facts was reflected in decreasing sales, which themselves provided a clear but urgent signal to William Lyons that the time had come for the company to invest in a new production car.

Considering the fact that, in the 1950s, Heynes and his team had spent much of their working lives immersed in the ideals of sports racing cars, it came as no surprise to find that their next production car embodied many characteristics of that genre. As mentioned earlier, the 1953 'C/D' prototype of the D-Type bore a strong resemblance to the model that would appear seven years later, and indeed the E-Type shared much in common with the D-Type itself.

After the disastrous accident at Le Mans in 1955 it was thought that future racing cars would be restricted to three litres, and Jaguar consequently decided to design a smaller car that could serve as both a Le Mans racer and a high-performance road car. Thus, Malcolm Sayer began design work on a prototype, incorporating the aerodynamic principles that had featured so strongly in the D-Type. The first prototype's monocoque was built of aluminium, and ahead of the front bulkhead a tubular sub-frame supported the engine, the steering and front suspension. The rear suspension differed from that in the D-Type, however, and this first prototype, known as E1A ('A' for aluminium), incorporated independent rear suspension that was mounted on a separate sub-frame and featured inboard disc brakes. Weighing 17cwt, the car was indeed a lightweight, and with its 3.8-litre engine was capable of 0-60 in 10½ seconds and a top speed of around 130mph. The second prototype, the E2A, was lent to Briggs Cunningham for Le Mans in 1960, and performed well until piston trouble forced its early retirement from the race.

The roadster styling had not escaped the notice of master sheet-metal

An early pre-production E-Type on test at MIRA. Benefiting from lighter and aerodynamically superior bodywork the first production cars were capable of 150mph.

For the first five years of its life the E-Type was strictly a two-seater, but in deference to families with children a 2+2 version was introduced in 1968. The bodywork was stretched by 8 inches to accommodate two rear seats for children, or for adults on short journeys.

Daimler Aquisition

In 1960, and with the emergence of the E-Type on the horizon, the Jaguar factory once again found itself desperately in need of more space, and this time was able to expand through the acquisition of Daimler and its factory in Radford, Coventry, having already purchased one of the Daimler wartime "shadow" factories at Browns Lane shortly after the war.

Together with the space, Jaguar inherited a wide range of vehicles, including limousines, buses and lorries. The Daimler Company was Britain's oldest car manufacturer, having been established in 1893 by Frederick Richard Simms. In 1910 Daimler had merged with B.S.A., and during World War I produced ambulances, lorries, staff cars, and cross-country tractors (forerunners of the armoured tank). Daimler underwent another merger in 1931, this time with Lanchester.

After World War II the Daimler range expanded successfully and, following the purchase of Daimler, Jaguar continued to build up the sales of buses, lorries and limousines, although the proud name of Daimler lost its individual character to become badge-engineered Jaguar versions.

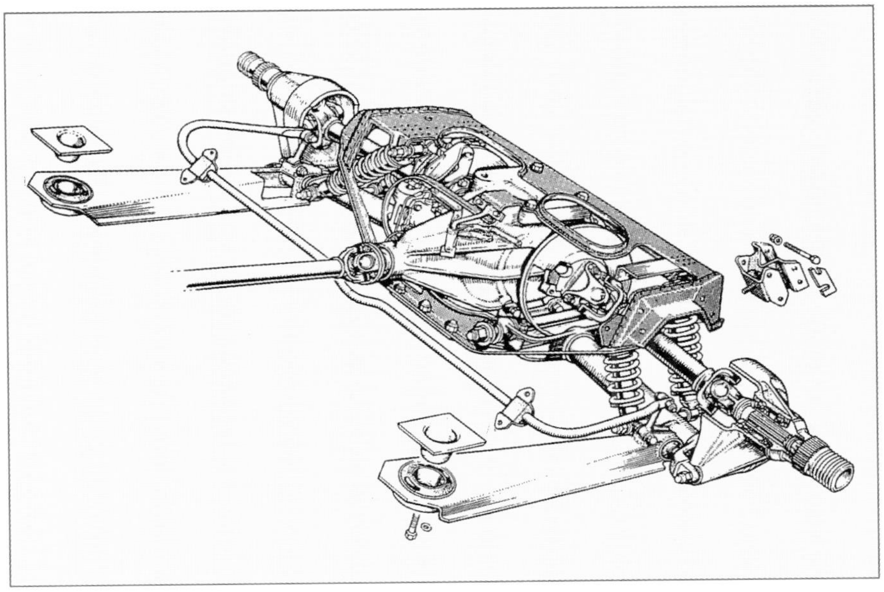

Independent rear suspension (IRS) contributed to the significant improvement in ride and road holding, which in conjunction with the XK engine and disk brakes made the E-Type such an enjoyable car to drive. A derivative of the IRS unit lives on in the XJS some 35 years later.

craftsman Bob Blake, a close colleague of Malcolm Sayer. Using welding rods, Blake mocked-up a fastback frame on one of the roadsters and then, whilst he and his colleagues were admiring the results of his fertile imagination, Lyons walked into the experimental shop. After some while in consideration, the Chairman announced: "It's good. We'll make it".

A number of other prototypes were built and tested until Jaguar took the plunge and launched the new E-Type at the Geneva Motor Show in 1961. If ever the word 'sexy' could be applied to a man-made object on four wheels, then this was it, and representatives of the world's motoring press

The interior of an early Mark I Roadster, less luxurious than the usual Jaguar standard but in keeping with the E-Type's sporty image. Note the symmetry of the layout for easy conversion to left-hand drive.

scrambled over one another to get a better view of the thrilling and sensuous exhibit. Outside demonstrations served to further impress potential customers, who were even given to forging invitations in order to secure a ride in one of the new models. Although the first customers were actually chosen by Jaguar, pop singers, film stars and even royalty fought for places in the order book; Lew Grade even wanted to borrow one for *The Saint* television series.

The E-Type was first introduced in roadster and fixed head coupé forms. The Roadster, or Open version, was a two-seater with a folding hood, although a hard-top version was also available; the Fixed Head, with a fastback roof and tailgate, was also a two-seater but possessed more luggage space. Even in the early 1960s, the prices of £2,098 and £2,197 respectively for the Roadster and Fixed Head represented excellent value for money, and undercut the Aston Martin DB4, the E-Type's closest rival, by a third.

In Britain the new E-Type's reputation spread rapidly with the staging of several road tests, the Fixed Head enthralling spectators with a top speed

Far Left Working on a Series I engine at the Browns Lane factory. The gold-painted head identifies the engine as a high-compression model.

Right Series I 4.2 Fixed Head Coupés in production. The car in the foreground is a 2+2, and the year probably 1966 or 1967.

Below The Series II was introduced in 1968 and included revisions dictated by American safety regulations regarding impact resistance and exhaust emissions.

that nudged 150mph. The 3.8-litre engine was the same unit as that used in the XK150S, but the E-Type's performance was improved by reason of its lighter and aerodynamically superior bodywork: acceleration from zero to 60 stood at an official 7.1 seconds. Such awe-inspiring performance was tempered with the renowned Jaguar attribute of tractability, and the new independent rear suspension bestowed the car with superb road-holding qualities and a very high level of passenger comfort. Any criticisms of the E-Type would undoubtedly emphasize the disc-braking system that was considered slightly inadequate for the model, and also the very size of the driver/passenger compartment which was often censured for being too small, a fact that reflected its origins in the racing car tradition of saving as much internal space as possible. Entry to the car was awkward over the high sills, the roofline was low, and space was at a definite premium between the steering wheel and the driving seat. In addition, gear changing was also found to be rather heavy, for there was no synchromesh on first gear, and the remaining three forward gears were sometimes a little sticky. These imperfections notwithstanding, however, the E-Type

Lightweight E-Type, chassis number 850666, owned by Peter Sutcliffe. Note the small plastic spoiler on the bonnet that helped to keep the windscreen clean during long endurance races. Note also the modified headlights which resemble the production specification for the Series II. Twelve of these Lightweight E's were produced with the aim of improving Jaguar's racing performance.

was a truly outstanding machine and probably the most beautiful sports car of the 1960s.

The twin-cam engine generated a considerable amount of heat, and to ameliorate this a double row of louvres was built into the bonnet just ahead of the windscreen. The long flowing bonnet sloped down to faired-in headlights covered by a plastic screen, although at that time covered headlights were illegal in the United States and the coverings were removed for the Series 1½ that was introduced in 1967. The original E-Types sported wire-spoked wheels with knock-off hubs, and cross-ply rather than radial tyres. To improve the efficiency of windscreen clearance at high speed, three rather than two wipers were employed, and sports cars exported to the United States also included this feature.

Very shortly after the model's introduction, Roadsters were supplied to the John Coombs and Equipe Endeavour racing teams for the E-Type's first foray into competitive racing, at Oulton Park in April 1961, where Graham Hill drove for Equipe and Roy Salvadori represented Coombs. Racing against 250GT Ferraris and a DB4GT Aston Martin, Salvadori surged into the lead only to be beset by braking problems, whereupon Graham Hill exchanged places and scored a notable win ahead of the Aston Martin driven by Innes Ireland. A short time later Salvadori led the field in an event at Crystal Palace. Le Mans was revisited in 1962 when a trio of privately owned E-Types joined the line-up, and although the event was now essentially the domain of dedicated racing machines the Jaguars performed admirably, with Salvadori and Cunningham coming home in fourth place immediately followed by Sargent and Lumsden. Despite these initial encouraging successes, however, it was clear that the E-Types were struggling against the lighter and more powerful Ferraris, and Jaguar sought to rectify these shortcomings by fitting a larger engine and all-synchromesh transmission.

The redesigned and enlarged 3.8 engine developed for the Mark X was also fitted into the 1964 model in a transition that did little to increase performance but offered a noticeable improvement in torque. The bodywork was basically unchanged except for the addition of chrome-plated emblems, but the interior had been considerably revised in the light of previous criticism, a footwell being added in order to facilitate access, and modifications to the rear bulkhead enabled the driver's seat to be moved further backward.

In continuing efforts to improve the performance of the E-Type in competitive racing, the John Coombs model was lightened further through the use of an aluminium-alloy bodyshell, that indirectly became the basis of the 'Lightweight E'. Built for independent racing teams, as well as an aluminium body these models possessed aluminium engine blocks, light-alloy wheels, a robust 5-speed gearbox and improved disc braking, but although they achieved moderate success against the Ferraris, the Lightweights were disappointing overall.

Whilst the E-Type had proved to be remarkably popular, the two-seat configuration represented obvious disadvantages for the family man who yearned for something a little sportier for that weekend outing. This matter

TOP The interior of a Series I 4.2, showing the newly introduced adjustable seatbacks.

BOTTOM The 4.2 Fixed Head Coupés introduced in 1964 were virtually unchanged externally.

Briggs Cunningham

Briggs Cunningham was a Californian millionaire sportsman who built his own racing sports cars incorporating the huge Chrysler V8 engine. In the early 1950s he was negotiating with Dunlop to supply his cars with their new disc brakes, but the company withdrew from negotiations at the last minute. At Le Mans in 1952, however, Jaguar C-Types (the only cars in the race to be fitted with disc brakes) took first, second and fourth places, the third place going to a Cunningham, brakes notwithstanding.

By 1955, financial problems connected with producing his own sports cars led to Cunningham forming an American Jaguar team, similar to Ecurie Ecosse, and his top driver, Phil Walters, along with Hawthorn, won the 1955 Sebring 12-hour race. When the Jaguar works team retired from competitive racing in 1956 Cunningham relieved them of one of their D-Types, which his tuner Alfred Momo developed into a 3.8-litre version, and the car, driven by Hawthorn and Bueb, finished third at Sebring in 1957. Cunningham subsequently re-equipped his team with Lister Jaguars, and to good effect in the Sports Car Club of America championships in 1958 and 1959. Jaguar had been experimenting with a new car to replace the XK120, and the E2A prototype was built. Cunningham was lent this car for Le Mans in 1960, but it had to retire early because of piston trouble.

For the 1963 Le Mans race Briggs Cunningham turned to the E-Type, entering three Lightweights, registrations 5114 WK, 5115 WK and 5116 WK. "14" retired with gearbox trouble very early in the race, and "16", driven by Roy Salvadori, spun off the track having hit oil deposited by another unfortunate competitor. At 10.30 the following morning the sole remaining E-Type suffered brake failure at the end of the Mulsanne Straight; the front end of the car was damaged, but with parts taken from "14" it was repaired sufficiently to complete the race in ninth position.

The XK engine was enlarged to 4.2 litres in 1964 and had an all-synchromesh 4-speed gearbox that did much to improve the hitherto sluggish gear change. At the same time, the dynamo was replaced by an alternator. The main advantage of the larger engine was increased torque rather than greater speed.

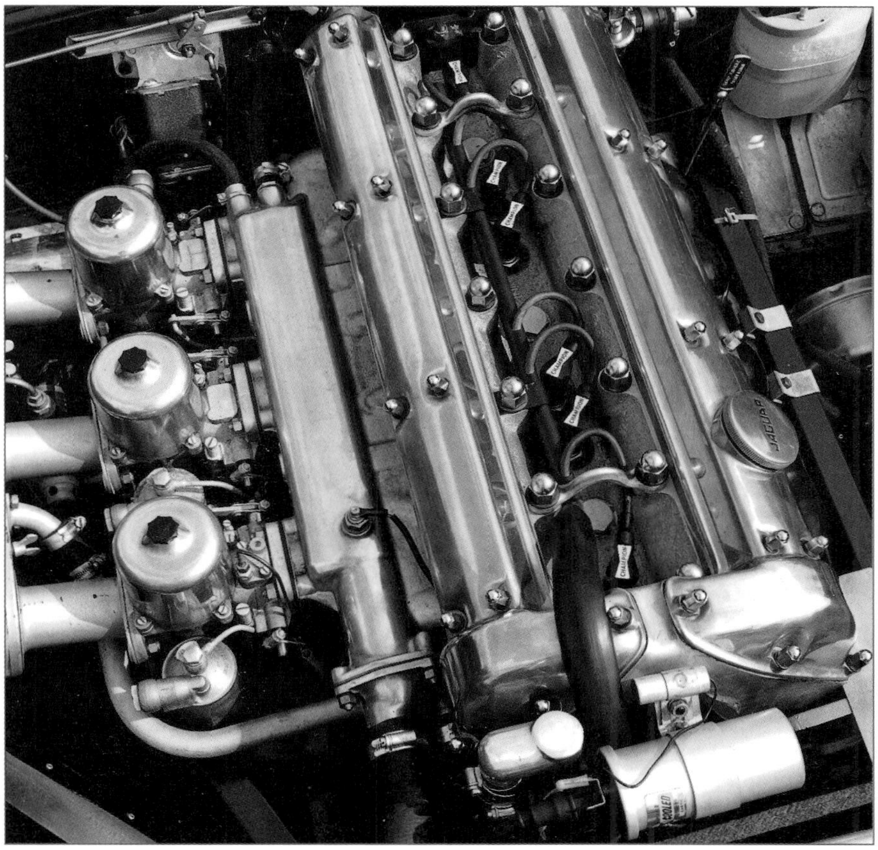

LEFT The Series II six-cylinder engine produced 177bhp and endowed the models with a top speed of 135mph.

BELOW Onlookers stand well back as this 1968 2+2 undergoes a quick modification! Conducted under strictly controlled conditions, crash tests provide invaluable information that can be translated into the structural improvement of future models.

Malcolm Sayer

Malcolm Sayer joined Jaguar in 1950, having spent some time at the Bristol Aircraft Company where he learnt the aerodynamic principles of flight. He was able to use these theories to good effect whilst designing several notable Jaguar cars, the first of these being the C-Type. Using wind tunnels to test his theories, his designs incorporated attractive styling and sweeping aerodynamic curves, qualities that undoubtedly helped to achieve the victories at Le Mans.

The D-Type the 'aircraft on wheels' that followed was also built to Sayer's wind-cheating design, and included improvements such as a novel plexiglass wrap-round windscreen, but perhaps the most memorable element was the stunning tailfin that was added to assist high-speed stability.

Sayer will be remembered predominantly for his design of the E-Type, which was probably the most beautiful sports car of the 1960s. He died in the 1970s whilst working on a design for a mid-engined production car.

was addressed in the spring of 1966 by the introduction of the 2+2 Fixed Head Coupé, the extra length being achieved by stretching the wheelbase by nine inches and the overall length by eight inches, factors that reduced the E-Type's top speed to around the 135mph mark. The extra space permitted the fitting of a pair of rear seats, intended for children, or for adults on short journeys. The 2+2 model was noticeable particularly for its higher roofline, taller and more-upright windscreen, and the addition of chrome trim under the side windows. The rear springs were strengthened to offset the additional 2cwt in overall weight which, in concert with the increased length, allowed Jaguar to offer optional automatic transmission for the first time on an E-Type, a feature also intended to attract overseas customers.

In the mid 1960s the United States introduced stringent and wide-

ranging emissions and safety regulations that applied to domestic production cars and imported models. Jaguar was not alone in having to conform, and in 1967 all three models of the E-Type (known as the XKE in the United States) were changed in order to meet the dictates of the US Federal Regulations. Twin electric fans were fitted and exhaust emissions were controlled in order to comply with the strict anti-pollution measures, and exported cars featured Stromberg carburettors in place of the triple SU's used for the British market. The interim Series 1½, as it was known, incorporated certain changes, depending on the country to which the model was exported, and from this point all pre-1967 models were known as Series I, and later models as Series II.

The changes demanded for the export market were also manifested in the Series II models that appeared in 1968, and cannot be said to have mproved

The Series III E-Type was the first car to receive the new V12 engine. Also known as the V12E, the Series III was considerably revised, acquiring a front grille and flared wheel arches in a bid to boost flagging E-Type sales.

E-TYPE OPEN TWO-SEATER

MODEL	Roadster
ENGINE	XK Twin overhead cam, 6-cylinder, 3781cc
MAX. POWER	265bhp
MAX. SPEED	149mph
PERFORMANCE	0-60 in 7.1 seconds
WEIGHT	24½cwt
LENGTH	14ft 7½in
WIDTH	5ft 4½in
IN PRODUCTION	1961-1964
QUANTITY	942 (rhd), 6,885 (lhd)
PRICE	£2,098

E-TYPE FIXED HEAD COUPÉ

MODEL	Closed Two-Seater
ENGINE	XK Twin overhead cam, 6-cylinder, 3781cc
MAX. POWER	265bhp
MAX. SPEED	150.4mph
PERFORMANCE	0-60 in 6.9 seconds
WEIGHT	25½cwt
LENGTH	14ft 7½in
WIDTH	5ft 4½in
IN PRODUCTION	1961-1964
QUANTITY	1,798 (rhd), 5,871 (lhd)
PRICE	£2,197

E-TYPE 4.2 FIXED HEAD COUPÉ AND OPEN TWO-SEATER

MODEL	Closed and Open two-seater
ENGINE	XK Twin overhead cam, 6-cylinder, 4235cc
MAX. POWER	265bhp
MAX. SPEED	150mph (FHC)
PERFORMANCE	0-60 in 7 seconds (FHC)
WEIGHT	24½cwt (Open), 25½cwt (FHC)
LENGTH	14ft 7½in
WIDTH	5ft 4½in
IN PRODUCTION	1964-1968
QUANTITY	9,550 (Open), 7,770 (FHC)
PRICE	£1,934 (Open), £2,033 (FHC)

E-TYPE 2+2

MODEL	Closed Two/Four Seater
ENGINE	XK Twin overhead cam, 6-cylinder, 4235cc
MAX. POWER	265bhp
MAX. SPEED	136.2mph (automatic)
PERFORMANCE	0-60 in 8.9 seconds (automatic)
WEIGHT	27½cwt
LENGTH	15ft 4½in
WIDTH	Not available
IN PRODUCTION	1966-1968
QUANTITY	5,600
PRICE	£2,245 (automatic £2,402)

SERIES II E-TYPE OPEN, FIXED HEAD COUPÉ AND 2+2

MODEL	Roadster, Closed Two-Seater and Closed Two/Four-Seater
ENGINE	XK Twin overhead cam, 6-cylinder, 4235cc
MAX. POWER	177bhp
MAX. SPEED	135mph
PERFORMANCE	Not available
WEIGHT	24½cwt (Open), 25½cwt (FHC) 27½cwt (2+2)
LENGTH	14ft 7½in (Open and FHC) 15ft 4½in (2+2)
WIDTH	5ft 4½in
IN PRODUCTION	1968-1970
QUANTITY	8,630 (Open), 4,860 (FHC) 5,330 (2+2)
PRICE	£2,117 (Open), £2,225 (FHC) £2,458 (2+2)

SERIES III E-TYPE OPEN TWO-SEATER AND 2+2

MODEL	Roadster and Closed Two/Four-Seater Coupé
ENGINE	V12 5343cc
MAX. POWER	272bhp
MAX. SPEED	146 and 142mph
PERFORMANCE	0-60 in 6.4 and 6.8 seconds
WEIGHT	28½cwt (Open), 29cwt (FHC)
LENGTH	15ft 4in
WIDTH	5ft 4½in
IN PRODUCTION	1971-1975 (OPEN), 1971-1973 (FHC)
QUANTITY	7,990 (Open), 7,300 (FHC)
PRICE	£3,139 (Open), £3,387 (FHC)

Above For some time Jaguar had been considering the development of a new engine to liven up sales of the E-Type, particularly in America. Being comparatively rare, the V12 was considered ideal and was built in single cam form.

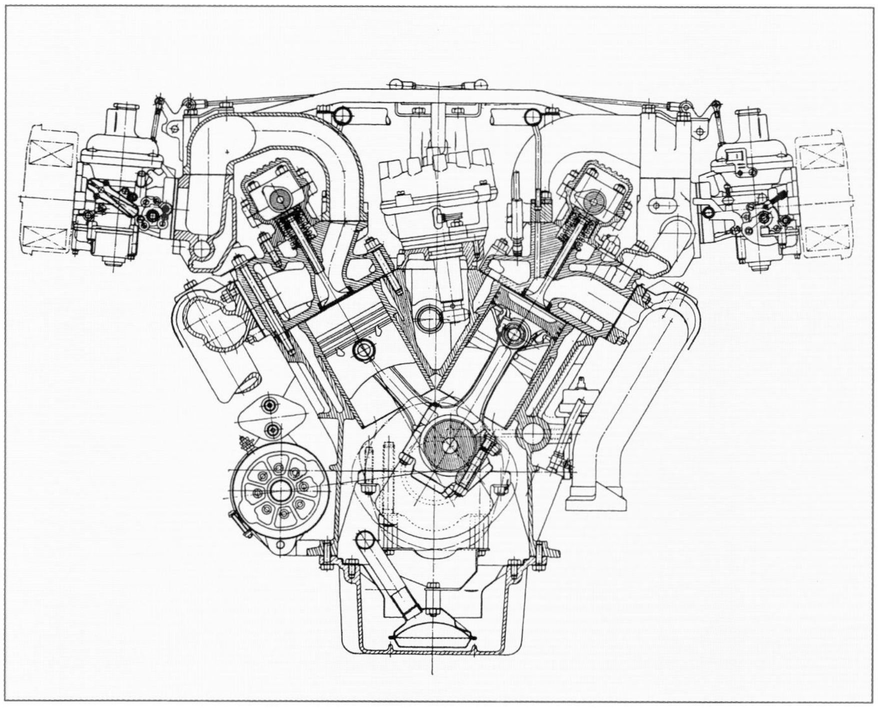

Right A cross-section of the new 60-degree V12 engine.

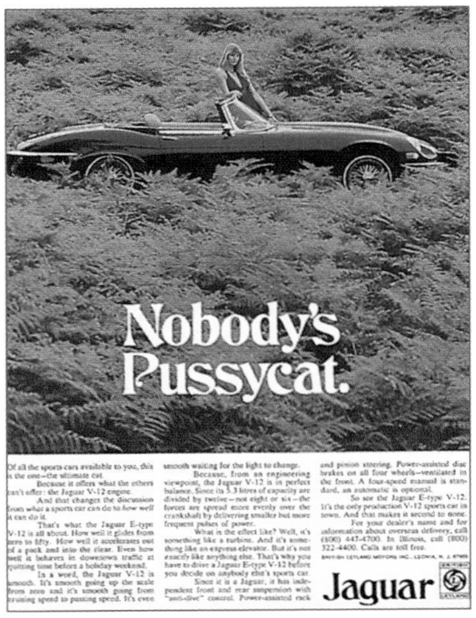

ABOVE Jaguar advertising, controversial at the time and undoubtedly politically incorrect in the 1990s, was as stylish and sexy as the cars it was hoping to sell.

BELOW Group 44 in America gave sales of the E-Type a boost by successfully racing V12 versions. Note the British Leyland ownership tag.

the glorious contours of the original E-Type. Apart from removal of the headlight covers and fitting of larger sidelight units front and rear, the bonnet mouth was remodelled to benefit cooling as well as to support the new option of air conditioning. The restyled bumpers were particularly prominent, the rear bumper comprising a new three-piece wrap-round item positioned higher to permit the siting of a square numberplate. Nor had the interior escaped the remodeller's hand, for the door handles were now recessed into the frame, and the original dashboard toggle switches were replaced by rocker switches. Despite the number and effect of these modifications, however, the most conspicuous element was the angle of the windscreen, the base of which was moved forward to increase the rake by 7 degrees. Accompanying the visual transformation were several important mechanical improvements, the most significant being the adoption of Girling caliper brakes; power steering was also available as an optional extra. The compulsory adoption of modifications to appease safety and pollution regulations also affected the amount of engine power that could be used, and resulted in a reduction in performance to between 130 and 135mph.

For some time Jaguar had been considering a new engine that could be shared both by production cars and racing types, and the likely candidate was either a V8 or a V12. The former unit was common in United States production cars but was known to possess a number of technical problems, whereas the V12 was not in widespread use although it featured strongly in the Italian Lamborghini and Ferrari stables. So in a bid to beat their rivals Jaguar made a bold statement by opting for the V12, not least for the reasons of simplicity, cost and weight.

In the mid 1960s Jaguar produced the XJ13, a single mid-engined

The last fifty V12 E-Types were all painted black except one that was painted green for a Jaguar collector. They all carried a plaque that was signed by Sir William Lyons and fixed to the dashboard. This V12 Roadster, registration HDU 555N, was the last one to be manufactured and was never sold. It now resides in Jaguar's own collection.

prototype that was fitted with a V12 engine and embodied the eclectic design qualities of the C-, D- and E-Types, but the engine was intended mainly for a new range of Jaguar saloons for the late 1960s, and as yet unannounced. So for the twin reasons of proving the new engine while at the same time boosting the flagging fortunes of the E-Type, a decision was made to fit the V12 in the Series III, or V12E, models introduced in 1971. Series III cars were noticeably different in their appearance: flared wheel arches were added to the wings in order to cover the wider tyres, and a larger grille was fitted in the bonnet mouth to reduce the heat generated by the 5.3-litre engine. Offered in Roadster and Fixed Head Coupé forms, the Open model was based on the same longer wheelbase as the Fixed Head and featured power steering as standard, whilst automatic transmission was now available as a result of the increased length.

The Series III models were well received and between 1971 and 1974 over 15,000 were made, 75 per cent of them for export. Although the Fixed Head was taken out of production in 1973 the Roadster was sold until early 1975, after which time Jaguar found itself without a dedicated open sports car for the first time since the late 1940s.

The Experimental XJ13

By 1964 sports car racing was becoming the kingdom of the wider-wheeled mid-engined cars and the E-Types were finding themselves increasingly uncompetitive. Jaguar had in fact been working on a V12 engine since 1955, and continued to develop an alloy engine that had a capacity of 4994cc and produced over 500bhp.

Fitted into a monocoque body (designed by Malcolm Sayer) that closely resembled that of the D-Type, the resulting car the XJ13 was unveiled in 1966 but was not entered for Le Mans that year because Jaguar was in the process of merging with the British Motor Corporation.

Unfortunately, development on the project ended in the late 1960s, by which time both racing engine technology and tyre technology had moved forward, and continued development would have entailed a number of expensive alterations to the prototype.

The mid-engine configuration prototype XJ13. Designed by William Heynes and Malcolm Sayer, it had an overhead-cam version of the V12 engine, and the body shape was an evolution of the C-, D-, and E-Types. Whilst being filmed on location the car somersaulted and sustained considerable damage. Having been rebuilt it was then housed in the Jaguar collection.

Chapter Seven

A Generation of XJs

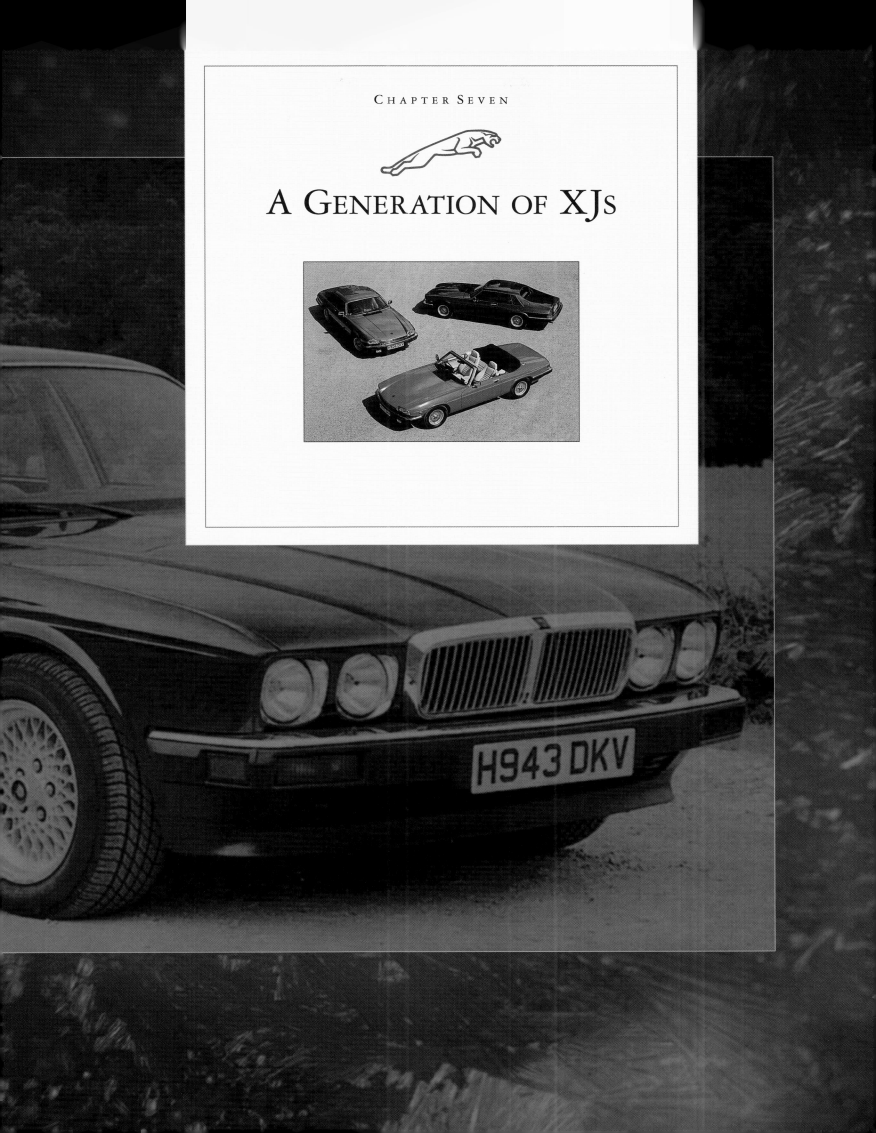

By the mid 1960s the Jaguar range comprised a veritable jigsaw of models in the form of the 2.4, 3.4 and 3.8 Mark IIs, 3.4 and 3.8 S-Types, and the Mark X saloons. The takeover of Daimler had endowed the Jaguar stable with buses and lorries as well as saloons and the SP250 sports car, and although the company wanted to succeed on the commercial-vehicle side there was a serious need for rationalization in the saloon car sector. Lyons had spent some time considering the options, however, and believed that his best solution lay in the introduction of a single model that could not only be powered by a variety of engines but also form the basis for any number of future vehicles.

In 1964, and in a bid to boost sales especially in the United States, the Mark X had received the revised 4.2-litre engine in a programme of improvements that included an all-synchromesh gearbox and upgrades to the automatic transmission, power steering and heating system.

In consideration of the S-Type's falling sales figures and with the introduction of the new single model well over twelve months away, Lyons decided to launch an interim saloon in 1967. Known as the 420 and powered by the revised 4.2-litre engine, this saloon had the appearance of the S-Type but was markedly similar to the Mark X in frontal view, a fact that particularly attracted export customers. As an interim model, however, production lasted only until the introduction of the XJ6 the following year.

Concurrently, and perhaps confusingly, the Mark X was renamed the 420G and was outwardly indistinguishable from its ancestor apart from the addition of a chrome strip along the sides, a large vertical slat in the radiator grille, and front spotlights that appeared in place of the former grilles. Inside, however, the dashboard now featured a padded roll as a safety feature along its top, into which was installed a small clock. The 420G remained in production until 1970, its last year of manufacture dovetailing with the XJ6's first.

In 1966 Lyons took the decision to merge Jaguar with the British Motor Corporation (BMC), a conclusion taken not only because he had reached

LEFT No expense was spared on the sumptuous interior of the XJ6, which was William Lyons' all-time favourite Jaguar.

retirement age, but also because his only son had been killed (while on his way to Le Mans in 1955) and therefore there was no natural heir to the Jaguar throne. At the time, BMC comprised Austin, Morris, MG, Riley and Wolseley, and was the largest car manufacturer in Britain. In hindsight, Lyons' decision has been viewed as unfortunate at best. With the notion that both parties would function independently, BMC and Jaguar were soon

Undoubtedly one of the world's finest saloons, the Series I XJ6 received instant acclaim when it was introduced in 1968.

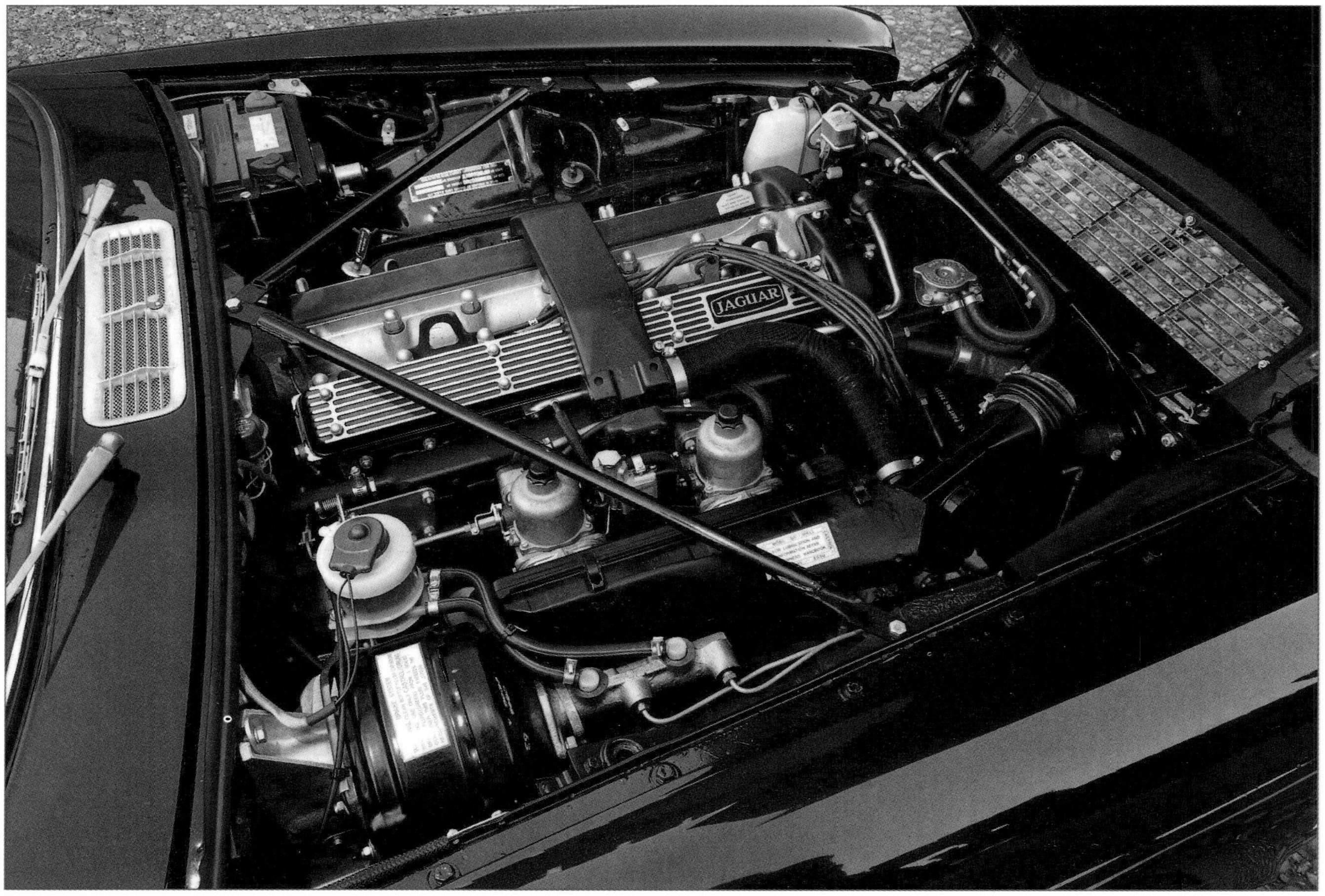

renamed British Motor Holdings, and the compromise worked well for two years until BMC, itself experiencing severe financial difficulties, was unable to resist a takeover by Lord Stokes of Leyland, and in 1968 the vast empire of British Leyland was established.

In the same year, the Mark II models (in production since 1959) came in for a modernization programme designed to squeeze a few more years out of their ageing design: the original 3.8 Saloon was discontinued, and the 2.4 and 3.4 models were renamed the 240 and 340 respectively. Although the 2.4's engine was uprated from 120 to 133bhp and received SU carburettors and both models received modern features such as slimline bumpers, signs of the times were unmistakable in the substitution of leather hide on the seats and the restitution of grilles in place of the front spotlights.

The single model that would replace Jaguar's confusing array of saloons, and one that undoubtedly represented the apex of Sir William Lyons' achievements and aspirations, was unveiled at London's Royal Lancaster Hotel in September 1968. The XJ6 embodied everything that was best about Jaguar and set new standards in refinement, comfort and handling,

TOP A fine view of the Series I XJ twin overhead-cam engine. In addition to the 4.2 version a 2.8-litre unit was introduced.

RIGHT The long-wheelbase XJ12 was launched partly in deference to complaints about the lack of legroom for rear-seat passengers, but it was a thirsty car and posed problems for owners during the oil crises of the 1970s.

Below This detailed cutaway shows the mechanical complexity of the XJ range, embodied in the form of a V12 Coupé.

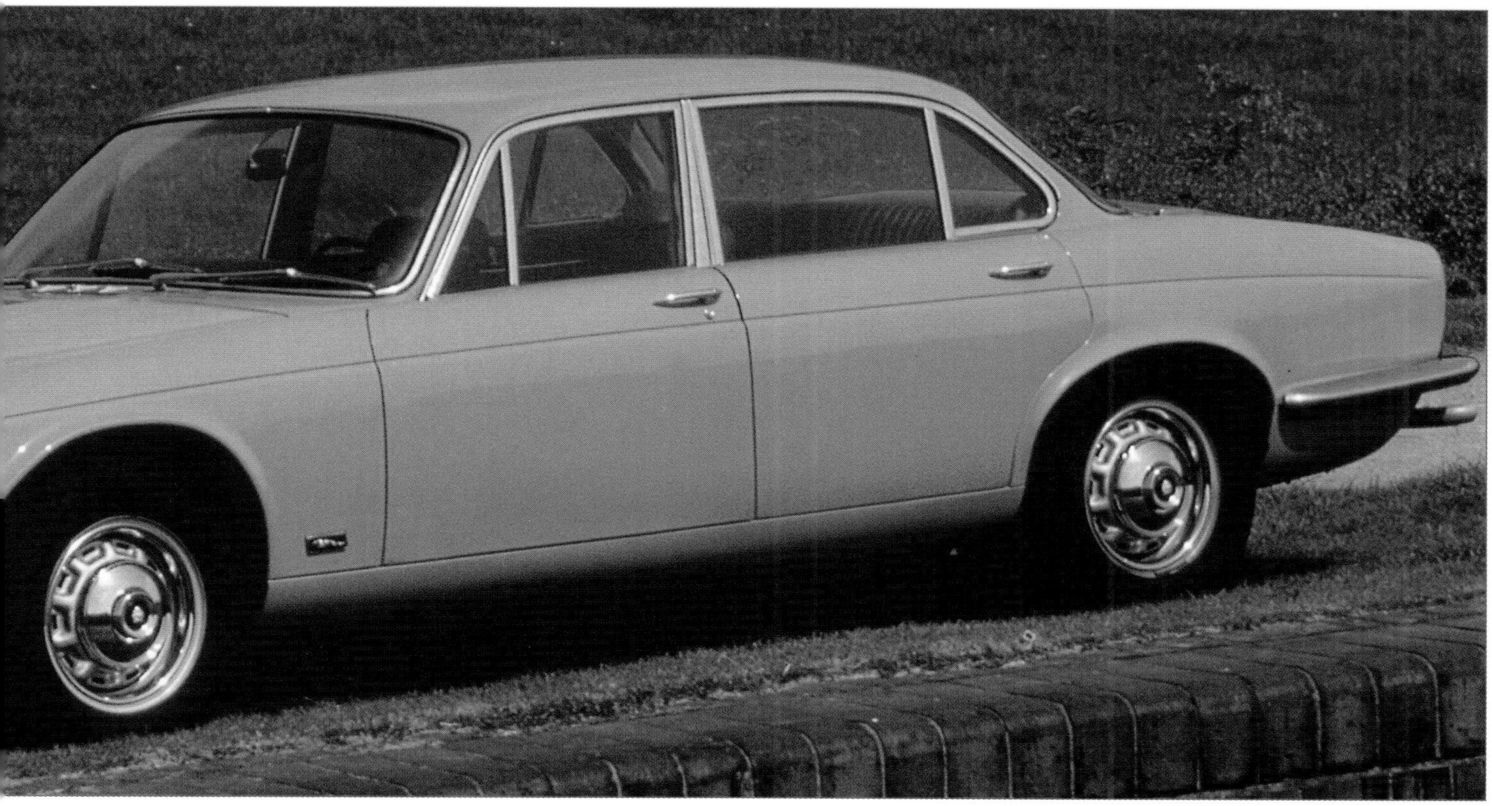

attributes that swiftly earned it *Car* magazine's prestigious 'Car of the Year' award. Within two years of the XJ6's introduction the S-Type was discontinued along with all remaining saloon models, and Jaguar concentrated on the E-Type, the XJ6 itself and its badge-engineered variant, the Daimler Sovereign.

The new XJ6 ('6' representing six cylinders) was the result of four years' design work by a team headed by William Heynes, and was a modern embodiment of the combined shapes of the 420, the 420G and the Mark X. With the V12 engine still some way from completion, the XJ6 was introduced with the 4.2- and the new economy 2.8-litre versions of the XK engine that were capable of accelerating this relatively heavy car from zero to 60 in eleven or 8.8 seconds respectively. Much attention had been paid to the quality of ride, and although a planned new rear suspension was postponed, the front assembly had been endowed with anti-dive characteristics to relieve tyre noise. The wide, low-profile tyres were developed especially by Dunlop, and whilst significantly improving roadholding characteristics they were inherently noisier than the earlier cross-plies.

The XJ6 certainly introduced new standards of luxury, and drew many and various superlatives from the motoring press and public alike: 'sporty, comfortable and fast' ... 'not too large, not too small' ... 'all things to all men'. It was, however, the last Jaguar vehicle to be created under Sir

The two-door XJ6C was particularly stylish. The absence of central pillars resulted in a very sleek appearance when the windows were lowered and the vinyl trim roof consolidated the sporty look.

William Lyons' auspices and it is timely, perhaps, to quote one of his own comments about his beloved Jaguars: "The product itself has always been designed to give the owner pleasure; I heard a story of one owner who found that the most peaceful way of gathering his thoughts and taking important decisions was to go out and sit in the cockpit of his Jaguar – without even having to drive it! That was one of the nicest compliments."

At the time of the BMC merger in 1966 Jaguar was testing the 'top-secret' V12 engine that was originally intended to power the XJ6, and the development team included William Heynes, Claude Bailey, Harry Mundy, and Walter Hassan, who in fact delayed his retirement in order to see the single-cam V12 engine into production. Its first home under the bonnet of the forthcoming XJ12 was delayed, however, when Jaguar became embroiled in the political storm clouds of the Leyland giant.

In the late 1960s Jaguar lost a number of its familiar figures. Arthur Whittaker, who joined the formative company in 1923 and rose from the post of sales assistant to become Deputy Chairman in 1961, retired in 1968 after a lifetime's service. The following year William Heynes retired from his position as Vice Chairman (Engineering) after over 30 years with the company, during which time he had established an engineering department that was unequalled in the motor industry. Heynes's vacancy on the Board was filled by Bob Knight and Walter Hassan. Yet another void in the Jaguar arsenal of experience was created in 1972 with the

The 'Big Cat' racing coupé of 1976. Note the spoilers, and also the wheel arches that were extended to accommodate the wide racing tyres.

More at home on the starting grid, the commanding presence of a Le Mans V12 XJ-S shows off its sensuous and feline form.

retirement of Walter Hassan himself, and he was succeeded by his assistant, Harry Mundy.

The XJ12 finally emerged in 1972 and was in immediate demand from all quarters, swiftly earning the 'Car of the Year' award and seriously in the running for the title of 'Best Car in the World'. Launched partly in deference to criticism of the XJ6's lack of legroom, the XJ12 featured a longer wheelbase. Apart from engine, transmission and cooling system there was little difference between the XJ6 and XJ12, although the latter sported a new radiator grille with a 'V' badge and an XJ12 badge on the bootlid. Powered by the V12 5343cc engine the XJ12 was capable of transporting its occupants at speeds of over 135mph, and the task of slowing them down was entrusted to ventilated disc brakes. At the time, and despite its size, the XJ12 was the fastest production five-seater in the world but had one disadvantage in its ferocious fuel consumption of

ABOVE The XJ-S Convertible benefited from the V12 engine and a two-door sporting body. When fitted with a Lucas fuel-injection system the XJ-S was capable of 150mph.

12mpg, a fact severely testing the theory that if one could afford to buy and tax an XJ12 then one could certainly afford the fuel. Owners of such thirsty cars were blissfully unaware that the theory was about to be tested even more severely, however, by a number of crippling oil crises in the 1970s.

The Frankfurt Motor Show of 1972 saw the unveiling of longer-wheelbase versions of both the 4.2-litre XJ6 and the XJ12 that were hurriedly produced by Jaguar after its rivals, Mercedes-Benz, had launched a 'stretched' series of its own. Produced primarily to afford rear passengers more legroom, these new models carried the suffix 'L' to denote the longer wheelbase. The original 2.8-litre XJ6 had sold particularly well in countries where insurance and taxation were based on engine size, but persistent piston problems led to its deletion from the range the following year.

ABOVE RIGHT The 3.6-litre engine sits comfortably in the engine bay of a Cabriolet.

RIGHT The 5.3-litre V12 engine was fitted into Series III XJs.

The Jaguar XJ-SC Cabriolet. Lynx Engineering produced its own fully-convertible XJ-S in 1978 well before Jaguar launched its own 3.6-litre XJ-SC.

The Series II XJs were introduced at the Frankfurt Motor Show in 1973 and featured several modifications. The most noticeable external differences were influenced by forthcoming US safety regulations that had necessitated the front bumper height to be raised, which in turn had required a new design for the radiator grille. The interior was completely modernized, with the dashboard layout revised so that instruments were grouped in front of the driver, and several functions could now be controlled from stalks on the steering column. Whilst effecting these compulsory alterations Jaguar took the opportunity to overhaul and update the heating/air-conditioning systems.

Announced at the same time as the Series IIs were the XJ6C and the XJ12C ('C' for Coupé) two-door versions of the short-wheelbase four-door XJ Saloon. In his last project before retirement in 1972, Sir William Lyons'

Above Folding hood detail of a 1983 Cabriolet.

Below The interior of an XJ-HE Coupé left-hand drive version destined for the American market.

elegant design had excluded the central pillars behind the doors so that the side windows could be lowered out of sight, an arrangement that created window sealing problems and increased wind noise at high speed. As a consequence of these setbacks production was delayed until 1975 after which time the Coupés were produced in relatively small numbers before the short-wheelbase concept was discontinued.

When Sir William Lyons retired at the age of 70 the position of Chairman and Chief Executive fell to 'Lofty' England, who assumed the mantle in the midst of an intensely turbulent period for the automotive industry. Since the Leyland takeover of 1968 the industry had been riddled with strikes and wage demands, and labour relations were spiralling

Martin Brundle in control of his XJ-S as he rounds a corner at Donington.

The experimental XJR-5 at work during the 1982/3 season. The car entered only a few races and was regarded primarily as a test vehicle.

A super-roadholding XJR-6, built by Tom Walkinshaw Racing (TWR). The team drivers found this model much easier to drive than some other comparative racing cars.

downward towards an abyss of self-destruction. After only a short time as Chairman, 'Lofty' England retired and moved to Austria.

To add to the motor industry's difficulties, the winter of 1973/4 witnessed a world energy crisis. Production of XJ6s continued unabated but sales of the XJ12 were seriously affected and forced Jaguar to make a number of changes to the range in 1975, including the introduction of a 3.4-litre 'economy' XJ.

In September 1973 Lord Stokes had appointed Geoffrey Robinson as Managing Director as the sickly British Leyland giant lurched from one disaster to another, but by mid 1974 Stokes realized that he had lost control of the unwieldy and unmanageable beast, and later that year the

Five XJR-9s were entered for Le Mans in 1988, achieving first and fourth positions. It was Jaguar's first representation at Le Mans for 31 years.

government had no alternative but to nationalize British Leyland. Sir Donald Ryder was appointed to report on the company's affairs; his findings, published in the Ryder Report, recommended that all management and technical teams be centralized, rather than devolved as Jaguar had been since its merger with BMC in 1966. British Leyland was renamed BL, and the whole Jaguar Board was disbanded.

One survivor of the Ryder recommendations was Jaguar Engineering, and in the aftermath of the maelstrom Bob Knight grasped the helm and furthered development of a successor to the XJ6, and despite a constant lack of capital Jaguar succeeded in launching the XJ-S in 1975. With the new policy of

The appointment of Michael Edwardes at BL led to increasing confidence at Jaguar and also to the introduction of the Series III XJs. An attractive and fresh style was achieved by the Italian firm Pininfarina in association with Jaguar's own design team.

sharing as many components as possible, the XJ-S (the hyphen was deleted in 1991) used a modified short-wheelbase XJ6 floorpan, the V12 engine and saloon suspension. Impact-absorbing bumpers were fitted front and rear, and the fuel tank was located in the front of the boot to protect it from impact. With its two-door sporting body the XJ-S was essentially a grand tourer, and with the magnificent fuel-injected V12 engine was capable of over 150mph.

BL experienced a period of increasing confidence and stability after the appointment of Michael Edwardes as Chairman, and he received a knighthood for his achievements. He was a man who understood and appreciated the value and efforts of individual companies as against the

Lynx and Jaguar

Lynx Engineering was established in 1968, over ten years after Jaguar's last win at Le Mans and at a time when the efficacy of historic Jaguar racers such as the C- and D-Types had been overtaken by the likes of Lotus and the Ford GT40.

Whilst enthusiasts could buy a D-Type, for example, and enter events like the Historic Sports Car Club races, obtaining spares was difficult and repairs often required the services of a racing specialist. Lynx Engineering, founded by Guy Black and Roger Ludgate, was set up to provide that authoritative help and advice and soon gained a considerable reputation for its expertise in the field of Jaguar sports racing cars.

Not long afterwards requests were made for Lynx to build D-Type replicas, and the company also became involved with development work on historic cars as well as BMX cycles and even airships.

In 1978 Lynx engineered the Lynx Spyder, the first of many 'independent' convertible bodywork conversions of the XJ-S, followed by the Eventer 'estate' and a performance coupé. Word travelled fast and the company was soon approached by owners of makes such as Mercedes, Saab and Porsche.

The classic car industry was one of the first leisure markets to be hit by the recession of the early 1990s and Lynx went into receivership in 1992. But all was not lost, however, as John Mayston-Taylor expressed an interest in the company, and after complex negotiations re-established it as Lynx Motors International Ltd.

Having followed a successful career in Canada interspersed with a five-year spell with Formula Ford in Britain, Mayston-Taylor was able to draw on his business experience and knowledge of racing as he set about restructuring the company. Supported by a loyal and dedicated workforce the company gradually regained confidence and planned new projects with a wide range of vehicles.

unwieldy and often unmanageable nature of vast corporations, and he restored a degree of autonomy to Jaguar by appointing Bob Knight as Managing Director. Despite this arrangement, certain sectors remained centralized and the British Leyland legacy manifested itself as Jaguar received components and bodywork that was often of appalling quality.

Despite the odds, Jaguar proceeded to replace the Series II models with the considerably updated Series III. The Italian firm Pininfarina was briefed to produce a new styling which, in association with the Jaguar design department, resulted in a pleasantly modernized design in which the roof was altered to give more headroom whilst also including a sunshine roof. Amongst a number of minor changes, the robust rubber bumpers of the Series II export models were fitted as standard. The Series III XJs

ABOVE Although produced by Jaguar, the Series III 5.3-litre XJ12 was also manufactured under the Daimler Double Six designation with appropriate refinements.

LEFT The interior of a left-hand drive 3.6-litre Daimler. The dashboard was endowed with a plethora of easily accessible controls, and the acclaimed standards of Daimler luxury are fully evident.

comprised the 5.3-litre V12, as well as 3.4- and 4.2-litre versions with five-speed gearboxes, the 4.2 also benefiting from fuel injection.

In 1980 and during the course of another strike, Sir Michael Edwardes appointed John Egan as Chairman of Jaguar. He came into a company that was losing almost £1 million a week and which had seen production drop from 30,000 to 14,000 vehicles per year since the early 1970s. Bob Knight had created an effective management team since his appointment as Managing Director but reached retirement soon after Egan's arrival. He was, however, offered control of the troubled and troublesome Castle Bromwich plant in Birmingham, a challenge that he readily accepted.

Following many hours of discussions between union officialdom and management the workforce returned and production recommenced: having

Bob Knight

Bob Knight first worked for Jaguar in the 1940s, when he was involved with chassis design. He was Project Manager for the C-Type, and in the field of development engineering was ranked as one of the world's foremost authorities. His legendary pioneering work with rubber mountings on the unitary construction Mark I saloons was later developed and led to refinement work on all Jaguars. Quality of ride and quietness of operation, both acknowledged features of Jaguar cars and the legacy of Bob Knight's earlier enterprise, were no better attested than in the XJ models introduced in 1968.

William Heynes and Bob Knight worked closely to develop new ideas, Knight designing the independent rear suspension that was introduced on the E-type and became a feature of every Jaguar model up to the XJ40.

Bob Knight fought British Leyland for Jaguar autonomy and independence during the wretched years of the early 1970s. After the Ryder Report he battled hard to keep Jaguar Engineering intact, and in so doing probably saved the Jaguar name from extinction.

After British Leyland's nationalization he was appointed Managing Director by Michael Edwardes, and for a few months he worked alongside new Jaguar Chairman John Egan before retiring in 1980.

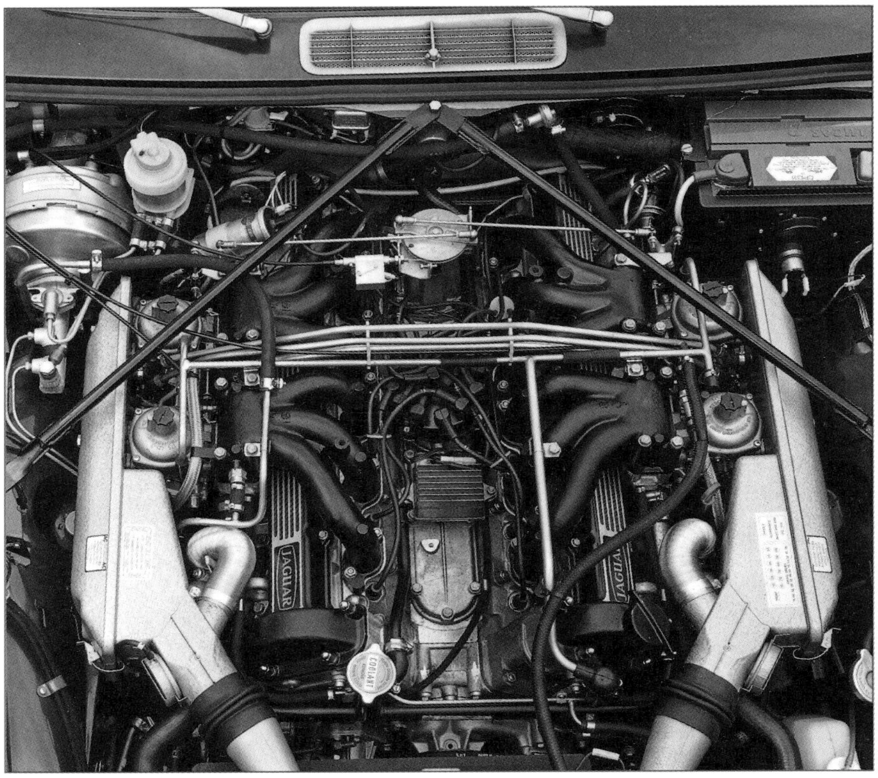

ABOVE RIGHT The impressive V12 powerplant of the XJ12.

brought an end to the strike John Egan then set about the task of recovery, and inaugurated a complete change of attitude within the company. A shrewd and ruthless businessman, he immediately identified the problems besetting Jaguar and at both Coventry and Birmingham instigated corrective measures that included strict quality control of workmanship and suppliers' components. The health of the company improved perceptibly, and quality was elevated to the point at which, in 1984, Liverpool Docks again witnessed the uplifting sight of Jaguar cars awaiting export.

During such turbulent times progress on the XJ6's successor was understandably slow, but Bob Knight and his team had persevered and had produced a mock-up of the bodywork which went before the BL Board for approval. The new styling received appreciable acclaim and prompted John Egan to convince both the Board and the incumbent Conservative government to invest an additional £100 million on Jaguar's future. The faithful V12 engine had also received attention and now appeared with new cylinder heads (developed by Swiss engineer Michael May); and with better fuel economy achieved through adjustment of the inlet and exhaust valve settings, the revised unit emerged as the HE (high-efficiency) engine.

The HE engine was fitted into the XJ Saloon and XJ-S in 1981, whereupon the Saloon became known as the XJ12 HE and featured alloy wheels, electrically-operated door mirrors, a headlight wash/wipe and a sunroof; fuel consumption improved to the value of about 20 per cent. The XJ-S was taken temporarily out of production in order to appease BL directors who wanted it deleted from the range, but John Egan stood his ground and was rewarded for his fortitude as sales of the XJ-S began to climb after it was fitted with the HE engine as well as alloy wheels, new Dunlop tyres, a chrome blade above the black rubber bumpers, a double

Group 44

In 1988 Jaguar once again won the 24-hour race at Le Mans after an absence of 31 years. The move back into racing proved troublesome and had begun more than ten years before, not in Britain but in America. As a result of the worldwide fuel crisis in the early 1970s, many V12 E-Types remained unsold, particularly in North America. In an effort to improve transatlantic sales, British Leyland supported an E-Type racing programme on the east coast of the United States, involving Group 44 under the direction of Bob Tullius.

In 1975, a year after the programme commenced, Tullius won the Sports Car Club of America National B Championship and continued to achieve excellent results. When the XJ-S was introduced Group 44 made some modifications to improve the handling of the car, and despite the XJ-S being a little slower than the E-Type, Bob Tullius gained the title of Category 1 Champion in 1977. A lighter version of the car was built for the 1978 season and Group 44 took both the driver's title and the manufacturer's title in the World Championship of Makes.

Group 44 continued to race heavily modified versions of the XJ-S, and by 1981 the Trans-Am rules had altered to allow more changes to be made to standard production cars. The 1981 season was not as successful as previous years, but thought had already been given to a completely new car for racing purposes.

The following year a prototype of a radical new design was unveiled, having been developed with the assistance of Jaguar by Lee Dykestra of Special Chassis Inc, in Grand Rapids, Michigan. The XJR-5 had a purpose-designed chassis with an aluminium honeycomb monocoque and steel bulkheads. Group 44 had several wins in 1983 before returning to Le Mans in 1984 and 1985, but without success on either occasion.

Toward the end of the 1985 season Group 44 introduced the XJR-7 that was aerodynamically improved, but it failed to win any races that year, and in 1986 Jaguar decided to entrust the running of the American team to the British company of Tom Walkinshaw Racing. Two years later Jaguar achieved its first triumph at Le Mans since 1957.

The V12 Series III engine was fitted with fuel injection from 1975.

coachline along its sides, and a bonnet badge. Jaguar also gave a nod to 'in-car entertainment' with the inclusion of a computer-based stereo system.

After only one year with John Egan in charge, both output and sales continued to increase and the company recorded a profit in the second half of 1981; the improvement continued throughout the following year and resulted in the production of over 22,000 vehicles. The trend was mirrored in the United States where sales rose from just 3,000 in 1980 to over 10,000 in 1982.

Whilst the V12 engine had been very successful, the heavy XK unit had powered its way through three decades and more and was approaching obsolescence. After much deliberation Jaguar decided to design a new all-aluminium engine in two versions: a performance version with the four-valve head, and an economy version with one V12 HE head. The new engine was known as the AJ6 (Advanced Jaguar six-cylinder) and first saw service in the lower-volume sporting car. A 3.6-litre AJ6 with the 24-valve head was fitted into the XJ-S 3.6, a model slightly reminiscent of the E-Type except for a bonnet bulge that was required in order to house the engine.

Slightly ahead of Jaguar, the firm of Lynx Engineering (a company with a considerable reputation for building and restoring D-Types) had introduced its own fully-convertible XJ-S in 1978. The Jaguar version, the XJ-SC, incorporated a 3.6-litre AJ6 engine and therefore featured the same bonnet bulge as the XJ-S 3.6. The open car was essentially a two-seater, the rear

MARK X 4.2 SALOON AND 420G

MODELS	Large Saloons
ENGINE	XK Twin overhead cam, 6-cylinder, 4235cc
MAX. POWER	265bhp
MAX. SPEED	122.5mph
PERFORMANCE	0-60 in 10.4 seconds
WEIGHT	37cwt
LENGTH	16ft 10in
WIDTH	6ft 4in
IN PRODUCTION	1964-1966 and 1966-1970
QUANTITY	5,119 (4.2) (plus 18 Limousines) 5,739 (420G) (plus 24 Limousines)
PRICE	£2,199 and £2,238

420 Saloon

MODEL	Medium-size Saloon
ENGINE	XK Twin overhead cam, 6-cylinder, 4235cc
MAX. POWER	245bhp
MAX. SPEED	123mph
PERFORMANCE	0-60 in 9.9 seconds
WEIGHT	33cwt
LENGTH	15ft 7½in
WIDTH	5ft 7in
IN PRODUCTION	1966-1968
QUANTITY	9,600
PRICE	£1,930

240 AND 340 SALOONS

MODELS	Compact Saloons
ENGINE	XK Twin overhead cam, 6-cylinder, 2483 and 3442cc
MAX. POWER	133 and 210bhp
MAX. SPEED	106 and 124mph
PERFORMANCE	0-60 in 12.5 and 8.8 seconds
WEIGHT	27/28½cwt
LENGTH	14ft 11in
WIDTH	5ft 6½in
IN PRODUCTION	1967-1969 and 1967-1968
QUANTITY	4,210 and 2,630
PRICE	£1,365 and £1,442

XJ6

MODEL	Large Saloon
ENGINE	K Twin overhead cam, 6-cylinder, 2792 and 4235cc
MAX. POWER	180 and 245bhp
MAX. SPEED	117 and 124mph
PERFORMANCE	0-60 in 11 and 8.8 seconds
WEIGHT	34cwt
LENGTH	16ft 2¾in
WIDTH	5ft 9¼in
IN PRODUCTION	1968-1973
QUANTITY	19,426 and 58,972
PRICE	£1,797 and £2,254

XJ12

MODEL	Large Saloon
ENGINE	V12 5343cc
MAX. POWER	253bhp
MAX. SPEED	146mph
PERFORMANCE	0-60 in 7.4 seconds
WEIGHT	34cwt
LENGTH	16ft 2¾in
WIDTH	5ft 9¼in
IN PRODUCTION	1972-1973
QUANTITY	3,220
PRICE	£3,726 £2,458 (2+2)

XJ6 AND XJ12 SERIES II

MODELS	Large Saloons
ENGINE	XK 6-cylinder, 4235cc and V12 5343cc
MAX. POWER	170 and 285bhp
MAX. SPEED	124 and 147mph
PERFORMANCE	0-60 in 8.8 and 7.8 seconds
WEIGHT	32cwt
LENGTH	15ft 9½in
WIDTH	5ft 9½in
IN PRODUCTION	1973-1979
QUANTITY	77,501 and 16,060
PRICE	£3,674 and £4,702

XJ6C AND XJ12C

MODELS	Two-door Coupés
ENGINE	XK 6-cylinder, 4235cc and V12 5343cc
MAX. POWER	245 and 285bhp
MAX. SPEED	124 and 148mph
PERFORMANCE	0-60 in 8.8 and 7.8 seconds
WEIGHT	Not available
LENGTH	Not available
WIDTH	Not available
IN PRODUCTION	1974-1977
QUANTITY	6,541 and 1,862
PRICE	£4,260 and £5,181

XJ6C AND XJ12C

MODELS	Two-door Coupés
ENGINE	XK 6-cylinder, 4235cc and V12 5343cc
MAX. POWER	245 and 285bhp
MAX. SPEED	124 and 148mph
PERFORMANCE	0-60 in 8.8 and 7.8 seconds
WEIGHT	Not available
LENGTH	Not available
WIDTH	Not available
IN PRODUCTION	1974-1977
QUANTITY	6,541 and 1,862
PRICE	£4,260 and £5,181

XJ-S

MODEL	Two-door Closed Coupé
ENGINE	V12 5343cc
MAX. POWER	285bhp
MAX. SPEED	153mph
PERFORMANCE	0-60 in 6.7 seconds
WEIGHT	33cwt
LENGTH	15ft 11½in
WIDTH	5ft 10½in
IN PRODUCTION	19751981
QUANTITY	14,792
PRICE	£8,900

The fuel-injected version of the 6-cylinder engine introduced in the Series II was carried over into Series III models.

seats having been removed to satisfy safety regulations. The original coupé body was redesigned to produce a Cabriolet that proved to be very attractive by reason of its performance and economy; in 1985 the Cabriolet also became available with the V12 engine.

Jaguar's fortunes had undergone a metamorphosis since the advent of John Egan, and 1984 was a year that both he and the company relished. Jaguar received the Queen's Award to Industry in April, and one month later the Conservative government of Mrs Thatcher, with its particular dislike of state-owned enterprises, took great pleasure in selling-off Jaguar to the public. The company was floated on the stock market and shares were oversubscribed tenfold. The day of privatization was indeed a thankful one for Jaguar as it returned to full autonomy once again.

In 1986 John Egan was knighted for his exceptional achievements at Jaguar, the company received the Queen's Award to Industry for the third successive year, saloon car sales continued to increase and orders were constant. Introduction of the long-awaited XJ40 replacement of the XJ6 had been deferred many times and Jaguar management was resolved to get everything right before the model's launch. Now under the project managership of Jim Randle, who had succeeded Bob Knight, the concept was studied and discussed in minute detail. 'Styling clinics' were run in Britain, Germany and the United States to assess all aspects of design, and between 1982 and 1986 over 5½ million miles of rigorous road testing was undertaken in order to appraise performance in every conceivable driving condition. Nothing was left to chance in the new model that would very soon carry Jaguar into the 1990s.

XJ220

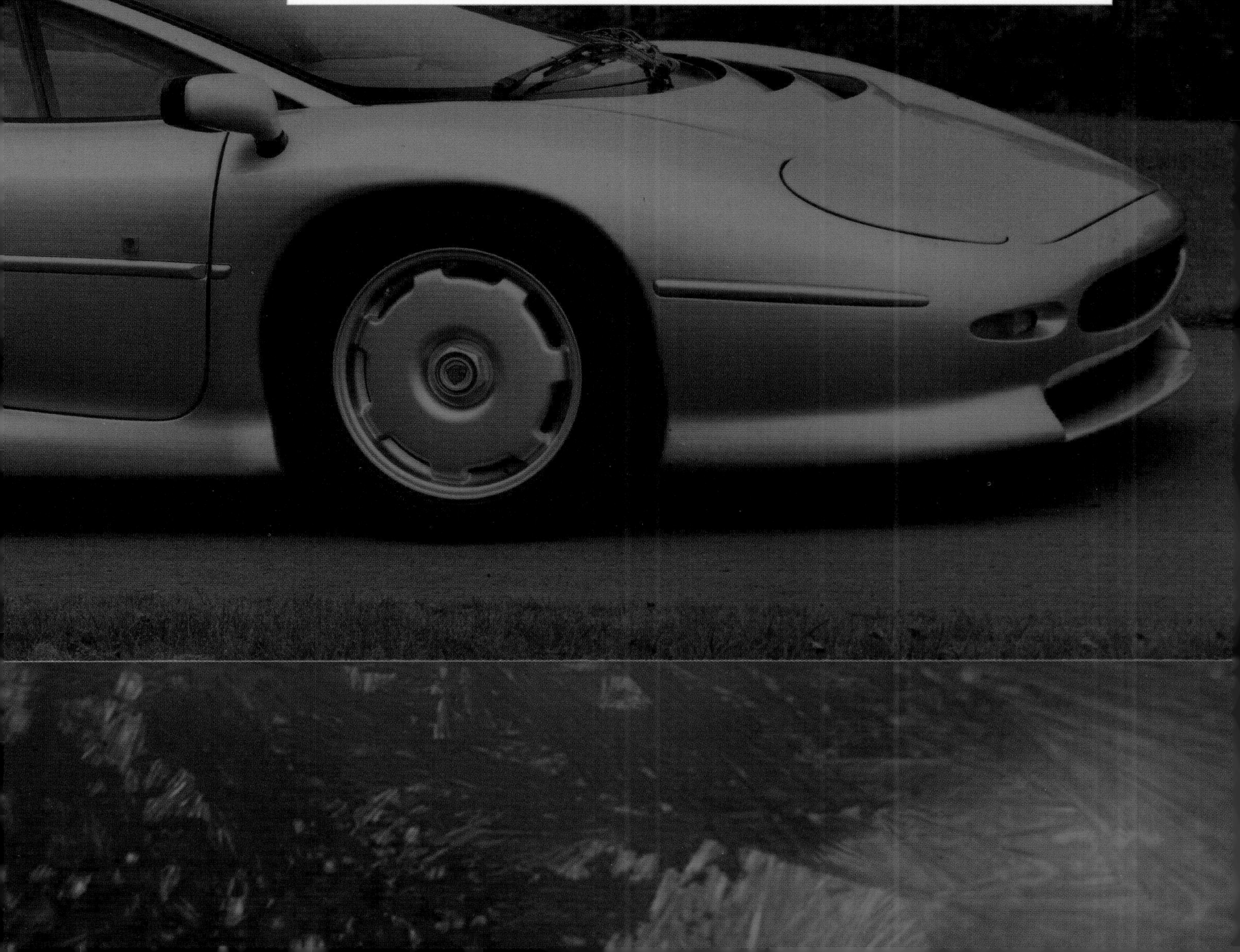

Chapter Eight

Models for The Millennium

In October 1986 the long-awaited XJ40 replacement of the XJ6 was finally introduced, although the new saloon did not officially carry the XJ40 code name and was commonly known as the XJ6. Though a brand new car it was evolutionary rather than revolutionary with an angular style that profited from superior aerodynamic styling, and was considerably lighter than its predecessor. Incorporating the latest technology the new XJ6 offered an innovative electrical system, new wiring known as low-current earth line switching, and microprocessor control and diagnostic systems. Voted 'Car of the Year' and lauded by the motoring press it was considered to be one of the most distinctive cars of its generation, and the £16,495 price for the basic 2.9-litre model was in fact less expensive than the cheapest Series III XJ that it replaced.

Two versions of the AJ6 engine were available: a new 2.9-litre economy unit with the May cylinder head, and a powerful 3.6-litre unit (that had been considerably refined since its introduction in the XJ-S three years before) with the 24-valve head. The XJ6 was the first marque to feature the new 'J-gate' transmission that provided the automatic transmission with a degree of override (a property that was later available on all Jaguar and Daimler cars), and both versions were offered with either automatic transmission or the Getrag manual five-speed gearbox.

Three models of the XJ6 were available. The first, a standard saloon, was supplied without features such as alloy wheels, air conditioning, cruise control or leather upholstery as standard, although these options could be specified by prospective purchasers. The Daimler Sovereign version of the earlier XJ6 had been discontinued in 1983 but the Sovereign label was revived for this model, which thus became the Jaguar Sovereign. This more luxurious option was equipped with the above features as well as anti-lock brakes, electrically operated seats and rear suspension ride height control. The third version was the even better-equipped Daimler model which boasted individualized interior trim and a distinctive chrome line along the bodywork. The Sovereign and Daimler models were recognizable by reason of their rectangular headlamps, whilst the standard saloon retained the circular four-headlight configuration.

Developed under the code-name XJ40, the long-awaited new XJ6 was finally unveiled in 1986. This symmetrical pattern comprises the new XJ6 and XJ-S range for 1991.

62 FKV
H676 FKV

More-advanced dedicated racing models were built after the XJR-9's welcome success at Le Mans in 1988. The car pictured is an XJR-14.

XJR-12s took first and second places at Le Mans in 1990 thus confirming that the 'Big Cat' had indeed returned to the racing circuit with a vengeance. The XJR-15 shown was a later addition to the family.

With the approaching 1990s Jaguar found itself with a strong model range and excellent sales figures, but profit margins were becoming a source of increasing concern due to the declining value of the dollar. A bombshell was released on 15 September 1989 when the Ford motor company announced its intention to purchase 15 per cent of Jaguar. The offer was firmly but politely rebuffed by the Jaguar Board, and a press statement declared that Ford's offer was "unwelcome". Soon afterwards General Motors, Ford's rival, made its own offer and one that Jaguar found difficult to withstand. Detailed and protracted discussions began, during which time Ford was itself purchasing Jaguar shares and seemingly intent on implementing a war with its rivals.

When Jaguar was privatized in 1984 the British government had instituted a 'Golden Share' agreement, an arrangement whereby the government could step in to protect Jaguar from any takeover bid made before 31 December 1990. In the event, Ford was permitted by the US government to purchase 15 per cent of Jaguar and in late October General Motors proceeded to buy the same, at which point the British government stated that it had no objection to shareholders wishing to cancel their

The solid and reliable AJ6 engine fitted in the XJ6, which was itself the first Jaguar marque to feature 'J-gate' transmission.

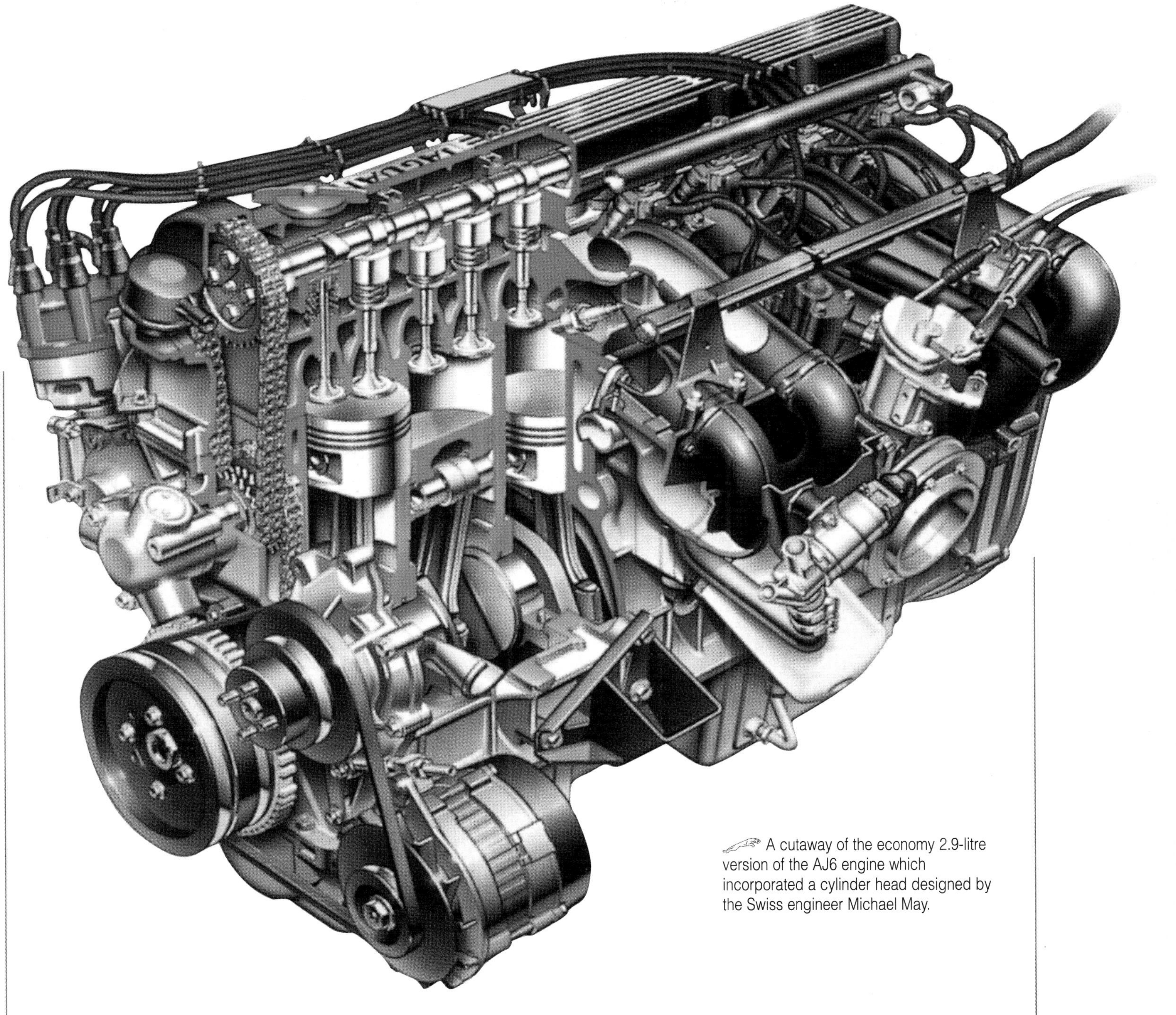

A cutaway of the economy 2.9-litre version of the AJ6 engine which incorporated a cylinder head designed by the Swiss engineer Michael May.

'Golden Share'. At a subsequent meeting shareholders were asked if they wished to cancel; the required 75 per cent of shareholders agreed, and the way was clear for Ford to proceed.

Ford immediately offered to buy out Jaguar for £8.50 per share, which cumulatively represented the $2.5 billion that the giant was prepared to pay, at which point General Motors relinquished their interest in the matter. Jaguar had no alternative but to accept the offer for an amount that even Ford admitted was probably too much but "worth it".

The Jaguar name lived on, however, and retained its own Board of Directors and autonomous financial control, with Ford injecting cash into Jaguar development projects and Jaguar having unreserved access to its new

Above 'It wouldn't be a Jaguar without the walnut and veneer.' Here, the tradition continues as veneered fascia panels are prepared by hand.

Left Sovereigns incorporated the very latest 'in-car entertainment' equipment as well as a state-of-the-art climate control system.

ABOVE Bet you've never seen one of these! A prototype estate version of the XJ6 was built for evaluation purposes.

LEFT The two AJ6 engines were joined in 1993 by a 12-cylinder version with which the new XJ12 was capable of 155mph. Distinguishable by its gold radiator grille, the XJ12 was also produced as a Daimler Double Six.

BELOW A convertible version of the XJ-S appeared in 1988 with overall cleaner lines. It featured an electrically operated hood that had necessitated a new front sub-frame and a number of other modifications.

ABOVE LEFT A bird's-eye view of the central console and controls of the V12 Convertible.

LEFT The example shown here is a 6.0-litre XJ-S of 1994. Only two years later the XJ-S marque was replaced by the new XK8 models.

Across -the-range engine improvements were effected during the lifetime of the XJ-S. The 6.0-litre V12 unit shown above appeared in 1992.

owner's considerable wealth of engineering, research and development facilities.

A number of modifications of varying degree were made to the XJ6 range in subsequent years. In 1990 the 3.6-litre engine was uprated to 4.0 litres thus greatly improving torque, and at the same time the dashboard bar gauge instrument was replaced by a traditional analogue unit. In the following year another engine change was effected when the 2.9 was superseded by a 3.2, and in 1993 a V12 was introduced when both Jaguar and Daimler models received a 6.0-litre upgraded version of the engine that had first appeared 22 years before. Concurrently, the XJ12 was given the four-headlamp configuration in preference to rectangular headlamps. The same year saw the introduction of the 3.2- and 4.0-litre XJ6 S, an appealing model with alloy wheels, more-rigid suspension and refitted interior. To appeal to the younger generation, and in a bid to allay the

Above The cockpit of the fabulous XJ220 Show Car complements the luxuriously appointed upholstery.

One of the world's fastest cars with a top speed of over 200mph, the XJ220 was initially priced at over £360,000. The XJ220C was a lighter version introduced in 1993 and three of these models raced at Le Mans the same year.

Above The sleek form of the XJ220 clearly shows the all-important cooling ducts for the potent engine.

Offer to Purchase

"Ford has been exploring actively opportunities to develop its presence in the worldwide luxury car market. The acquisition of the Company by Ford represents an important step towards fulfilling this objective and will, at the same time, strengthen Ford's existing substantial commitment to the United Kingdom.

"Ford and the Company believe that there is considerable potential to increase sales volume for the Company's product range in Europe, the United States and other parts of the world. Over the longer term, Ford and the Company expect to enhance significantly the Company's prospects and presence throughout the world through the joint development of new product and manufacturing ideas.

"To continue to compete effectively in world markets, Ford and the Company believe that the Company will need greater resources than it currently has. Ford and the Company believe that Ford will bring the following strategic benefits:

"substantial financial resources which will enable the Company to accelerate new product developments; and

"access to a worldwide technology base. Ford and the Company believe that there are substantial benefits to be gained for both companies in building upon the Company's history as a manufacturer of fine sports and luxury cars."

Taken from the 45-page document discussing the Ford's formal Offer to Purchase.

prospect of lost sales through the introduction of a 'new' XJ6 in 1994, the stylish and impressive XJ Gold was launched, which came with standard 'extras' such as a rosewood interior, diamond-turned alloy wheels and a gold-plated badge on the bootlid.

The 'new series' XJ6 Saloon was launched in 1994, the result of a project code-named X300 into which Ford had injected £200 million (£110 million of this being spent on the manufacturing process alone). The new marque was very well received by both the media and the public, record orders serving to demonstrate customers' confidence in the quality of engineering and performance.

Outwardly, the angular characteristics of its predecessor were smoothed out to further improve aerodynamic efficiency, and the front appeared more rounded with a restyled four-headlamp configuration reminiscent of earlier Series XJs. A useful and practical feature was the inclusion of a dashboard control by which the headlamps could be remotely adjusted to four positions. The AJ6 engine was replaced by the more powerful and more economical AJ16 alloy unit that had benefited from the inclusion of over one hundred new parts. Both the 3.2- and 4.0-litre engines were adopted in the standard, Sport and Sovereign vehicles. Power steering was included as standard on these heavy models, and a fully adjustable steering wheel was fitted for the first time. Ride quality was enhanced by inclusion of the optional ride-levelling suspension system to maintain the car's even disposition. The models were also endowed with a number of internal improvements aimed at the comfort of their occupants, and the boot spacious enough to take two sets of golf clubs accommodated the most up-to-date CD-player and amplifier equipment.

After the launch of the 'new' XJ6 in 1994 the best-selling model was the 3.2-litre Sport, reflecting the younger generation's level of interest in the

The ultra high-performance XK8 Coupé and Convertible sports cars were launched in 1996. Incorporating high-technology electronics and multiplexing, the Coupé version was capable of acceleration from rest to 60mph in 5.3 seconds.

marque. Saloon models received some criticism over lack of legroom for rear-seat passengers, a particular complaint from customers in the United States, and to address these matters Jaguar offered long-wheelbase models in 1997. In Britain these versions were known as Majestics, a fact that caused some confusion because some export conventional-wheelbase models bore the same name. Jaguar also manufactured a small number of Insignia models that were essentially custom made and often with unusual paint finishes.

Cars in the XJ6 series later appeared with either Sport or Classic styling themes and were in production until 1998. The XJ Sport 3.2 was powered by the AJ-V8 engine with five-speed electronic automatic transmission for a top speed of 140mph, and included a completely new interior design with

Sitting Comfortably

Jaguar has established a well-deserved reputation for quality and style, not least because of its classically styled interiors: wood veneers, thick pile carpeting and soft leather are all hallmarks of a Jaguar car. As modern technology has advanced, so too has Jaguar with its use of computer-aided engineering design for many components, including seats.

The quality of seating is a factor that can affect a driver's impression of the whole car. In the past the seat was styled first, and only then would designers work on the comfort factor. In the light of medical research into poor driving posture, and bearing in mind the fact that back problems affect approximately 20 per cent of the population and represent a primary cause of absence from work, Jaguar has given a great deal of thought to the function of the seat.

Most manufacturers design to a standard formula that takes no account of height or weight differences, but Jaguar has studied research data which highlights potential problem areas, such as the need for support in the lumbar region and lower thighs, and the need for foot pedals to be accessible without stretching. Its seat design has evolved, particularly through the Series III and XJ6/XJ40 models, and designers have established a set of measurements based on anthropometric averages, which form the basis of dimensions used during seat design. A technique known as 'pressure mapping' is used: the pressures exerted by a person sitting on a seat are interpreted on a computer 'map' in order to discover where most stresses occur and where support is needed.

Structural pressed-steel frames are now used for improved seat strength, and the most up-to-date dual density foams provide differing amounts of support within the same overall thickness. Computer-aided design is particularly helpful in decisions regarding cover styling and patterning, a task that formerly took many weeks of laborious work as the leather was cut and stitched onto a clay model, and then unpicked in order to provide an accurate pattern. Even with modern aids, however, it takes many months to implement a new design or change part of an old one, and considerable investment is required. Jaguar buyers are requested to complete a detailed questionnaire after they have been driving their new cars for a few months, and designers then act upon the information received.

Electric controls were introduced in 1986, mainly for height adjustment, and now the latest motor controls can raise and lower the whole seat, tilt the cushion and seat-back, move the seat backwards and forwards, raise and lower the head restraint, and operate a lumbar support 'bladder'. A memory can store three seat-position settings as well as door mirror and steering wheel positions; and in a touch that is truly a hallmark of Jaguar in the 1990s, when the key is removed from the ignition, the steering wheel automatically retracts and the seat moves backwards to facilitate the driver's exit from the car. In the latest model XJ8, thinking has advanced still further, and an airbag is built into the side of the seat. In the event of a side impact collision the bag will burst through the side stitching of the seat, and will always be in the right place to protect the occupant, whatever the position of the seat.

The latest 4.0-litre supercharged AJ-V8 engine produces a rousing 370bhp, although the S-Type saloon that is due to be launched in October 1998 will probably have the new AJ26 V8 powerplant.

Above Right XK8s rumble slowly but deliberately along the production line. When conceived in 1992 under the code name X100, Jaguar set out to produce the most advanced coupé ever made. The XK8's monocoque structure was entirely re-engineered but cleverly evokes its lineage to the E-Type.

an electronically controlled air-conditioning system. The heart of the Classic range comprised the 3.2-litre XJ6, XJ Executive and Sovereign, and the 4.0-litre Sovereign Long Wheelbase; the Jaguar long-wheelbase option was available on the XJ6 and Sovereign 3.2-litre cars. All models in the Classic range had a choice of transmission and numerous standard features such as electrically-operated windows and door mirrors, trip computer and custom-designed audio system; optional extras dependent upon model included electric rear seats and wood/leather steering wheel. A poignant sign of the times was recognized with the fitting in all models of a 'panic' switch for sunroof closing and central door-locking.

The Daimler V8 and Super V8 marques offered the ultimate refinements for motoring in the 1990s. The first, powered by the 4.0-litre V8, was endowed with the traditional finest-quality leather and walnut interior whilst enjoying the benefits of up-to-date technology with features such as seat heaters and electrically powered front seats with memory. The longer wheelbase afforded the space for inclusion of veneered picnic trays that

Greening Jaguar

The assembly lines at Jaguar are almost as quiet and smooth-running as the company's cars. In conditions of virtually clinical cleanliness, some of the most advanced technology in the industry is applied during the manufacture of each vehicle. But even before a prototype is built, however, computer-aided design is used to check and validate the performance of the components. When the design team is satisfied with its work, a large number of prototypes undergo evaluation in climates as diverse as the icy wastes of Canada and the parched deserts of Arizona, as well as on test tracks throughout the world. Prototypes are also subjected to controlled tests involving extremes of heat and cold and conditions of 100 per cent humidity.

Environmental considerations are of extreme importance. The AJ-V8 catalysts warm up to operating temperature in 30 seconds, the base paint coat is applied using technology that reduces solvent emissions by 85 per cent, and at the end of its life more than 83 per cent of the weight of each Jaguar car is recycled. Energy consumption during manufacture is also closely considered and monitored by computer-controlled systems.

In partnership with the Worldwide Fund for Nature, Jaguar helped to establish the first jaguar sanctuary in Belize, Central America, where strenuous efforts are made toward safeguarding the future of these big cats, that are now an endangered species.

The XK8 Convertible was announced ahead of the Coupé at the New York Motor Show in 1996. Significantly, the E-Type had made its debut at the same show 35 years earlier.

These diagrams show the oil and water systems of the AJ-V8 engine.

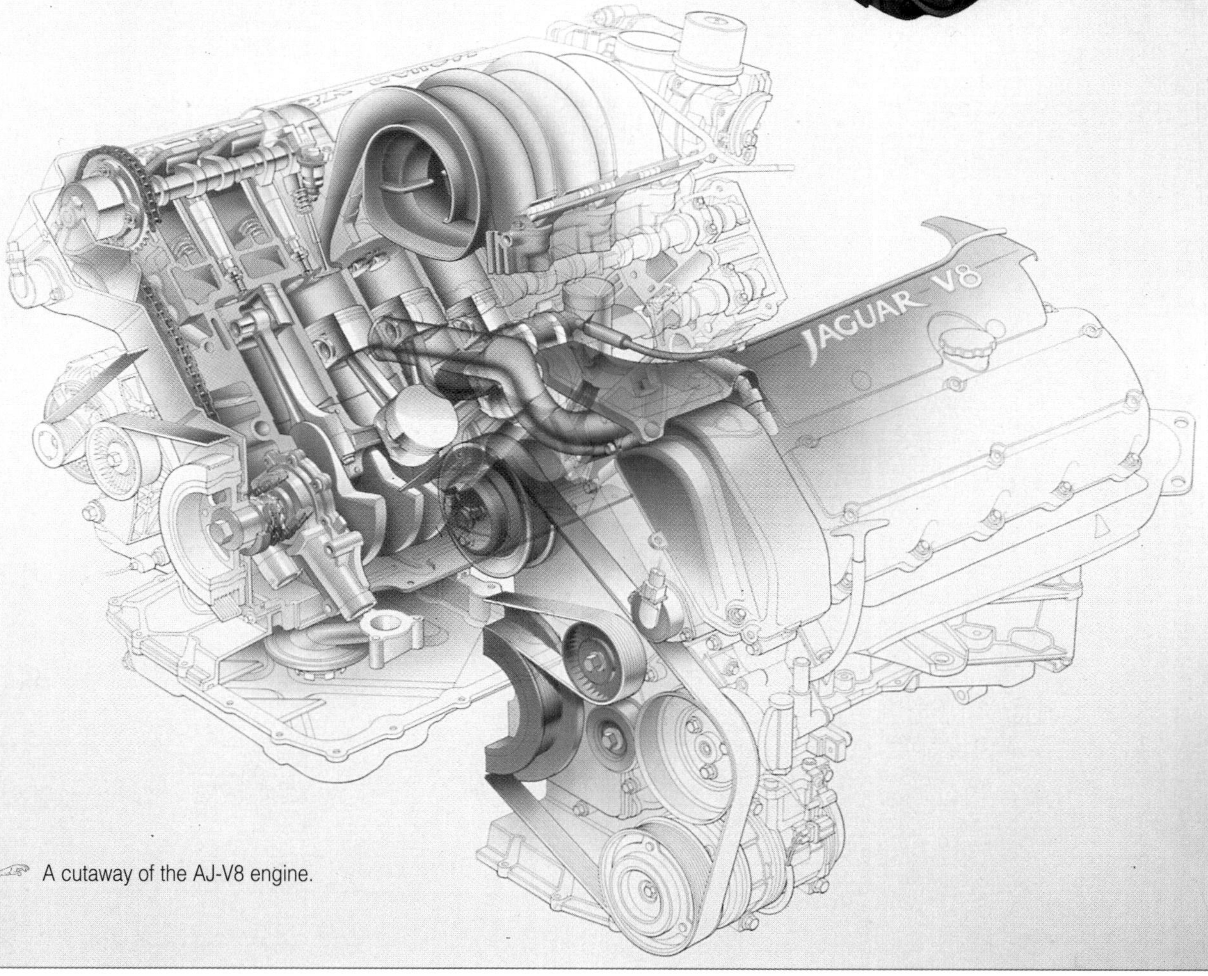

A cutaway of the AJ-V8 engine.

folded down from the front seat backs. The 4.5-litre Super V8 was bathed in luxury and possessed all the imagined qualities of limousine comfort whilst also benefiting from the electronic sophistication of the age.

JaguarSport, a joint business of Jaguar and the Tom Walkinshaw racing group, was set up in May 1988 with the objective of producing about 500 cars a year at Walkinshaw's premises in Oxfordshire. The overall creed of the enterprise was to manufacture cars based on the Jaguar range but with enhanced performance achieved through mechanical and body modifications. Unveiled in the summer of 1988, the first fruit of this project was the XJR-S Coupé, powered by the 5.3-litre 290bhp V12 engine and instantly identifiable by its body-colour bumpers and rear spoiler. Launched in the same year was the aptly named Celebration Coupé, a special limited edition of 100 examples in celebration of that year's Jaguar victory at Le Mans. In 1989 the XJR-S was fitted with the more powerful 6-litre V12 that conferred it with a top speed of about 150mph, and with the V12 uprated to 333bhp two years later the car was bestowed with sports car performance.

Launched in August 1988, the XJR was the JaguarSport version of the XJ saloon family, initially based on the 3.6-litre XJ6 and with automatic transmission. As with the XJR-S, primary modifications addressed the interior and handling qualities, but later revisions resulted in a distinctive black radiator grille, rear spoiler and body-colour bumpers. Minor improvements were made to the model in 1989 and 1990, but after that time there was less interest in the model and production was terminated in 1992.

BELOW A telescopic headlamp power wash is an optional extra on the XK8.

BOTTOM The cockpit of the XK8 preserves the walnut and veneer traditions of Jaguar cars.

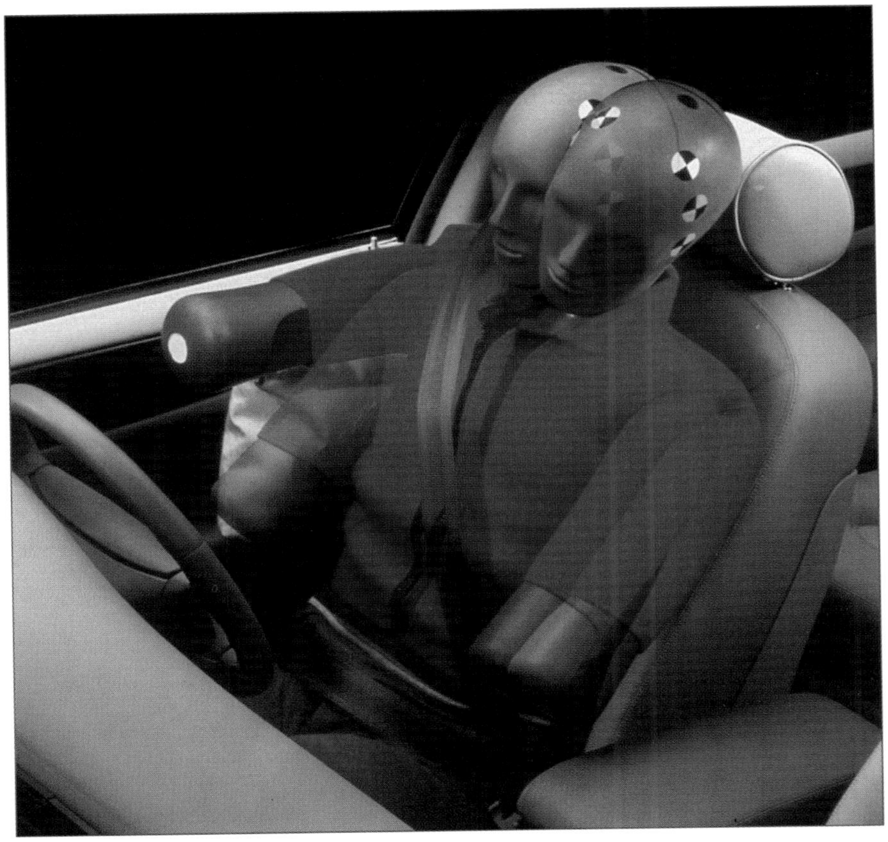

The Safest Car on the Road

For four consecutive years Jaguar cars were nominated 'Safest Car on the Road' by the former Department of Transport, an accolade earned from the results of police accident statistics. The body structure of a Jaguar car is designed to exceed worldwide crash legislation and is stringently evaluated in controlled car-crash tests. High-strength and zinc-coated steels in the majority of body panels together with high-strength steel beams within the doors combine to safeguard the occupants, whilst box-shaped longitudinal members that act as crush tubes to absorb impact forces afford additional protection to the passenger compartment. In the event of an impact the doors automatically unlock, and fuel and ignition systems shut down. All modern Jaguars have driver and front passenger airbags, and some models also include side airbags, microprocessor controls deploying the airbags immediately upon impact.

ABOVE The ingenuity of modern safety features matches the increasing electronic sophistication of modern cars. All new Jaguars include driver and front passenger airbags and some models include side airbags in their inventory.

Jaguar was the first motor manufacturer of modern times to introduce a supercharged engine into a luxury saloon. The new XJR, Jaguar's fastest saloon, can surpass the acceleration of many sports cars with its performance of 0-60 in 5.3 seconds. The supercharged AJ-V8 engine develops a stunning 370bhp that is delivered through a five-speed electronic automatic transmission unique to the supercharged engine. Conspicuous especially for its wire-mesh grille, the XJR incorporates Jaguar's Computer Active Technology Suspension (CATS) system that bestows the model with a combination of sports car handling and superb ride characteristics. Interior features include electrically adjustable leather-trimmed sports seats, a wood/leather steering wheel and wooden gearknob.

One of the world's fastest cars, the XJ220, entered production early in 1991 although a single prototype model had been exhibited three years before at the Motor Show in Birmingham. With the staggering initial price tag of £361,000 (prospective customers being requested to pay a £50,000 deposit), only 220 production models were planned. With due regard to the economic recession in Europe and America the price had been index-linked, however, and by the time of the car's actual launch customers were presented with a bill for over £400,000, a situation that forced many intending buyers to abandon their dreams.

Unveiled at the Tokyo Motor Show in October 1991, the XJ220 outwardly resembled the previous 1988 model although the wheelbase had been shortened by about 8 inches. Beneath the bonnet, however, things were radically different, the V12 having been replaced by the significantly more powerful 3.5-litre twin-turbocharged V6 that developed an incredible

Continuing the XJ Series towards the turn of the century, the XJ8 made its appearance in 1997, when this 4.0-litre Classic model was in the showrooms at £41,880 .

542bhp and endowed the new model with a top speed in excess of 210mph. In a complete revision programme the four-wheel drive of its forerunner had been substituted by rear-wheel drive, and features such as anti-lock brakes, adaptive suspension and scissor doors had not been included in the new package. Performance was improved still further with the introduction of the lighter XJ220-C in 1993, and three of these cars performed at Le Mans later in the year.

The appearance of Tom Walkinshaw's even faster XJR-15 in 1990 produced legal complications, as a result of which Jaguar announced that it would allow customers to buy themselves out of their 220 contracts. Production of the XJ220 ceased in 1994 after the appearance of 275 examples.

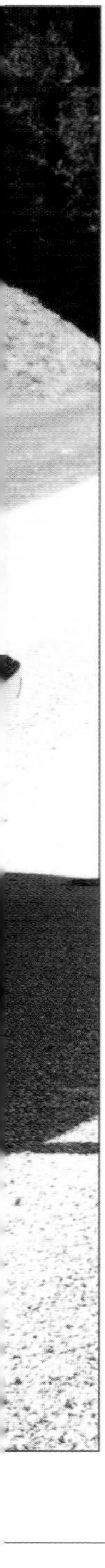

ABOVE Daimler V8 lineage on show as Majestic Major and Super V8 personify the ongoing style of Jaguar design.

The new XK8 range was launched in 1996, the Convertible appearing in April at the New York Motor Show followed by the Coupé's introduction at the Geneva Motor Show in October, after which both models superseded the XJS after a production life of 21 years. Indeed the XK8 was based on the platform of the XJS although 90 per cent of its components were carried over from the XJ Series range.

In its tradition of introducing new engine designs in sports car series, Jaguar set out to produce the most advanced coupé ever made. The brand new 4.0-litre AJ-V8 engine develops 290bhp and bestows the Coupé with a top speed of 156mph. The computer power driving the engine comes from two 15-bit microprocessors each of 98Kb, and the electronic throttle is capable of overriding the mechanical linkage to the pedal in order to assist smooth driving. Traditional wiring has given way to multiplexing whereby components and switches are linked by a power wire and a message cable that can distribute up to 700 messages per second. Switches send signals via the message cable which are recognized the component's control modules.

The XK8 is peppered with state-of-the-art features such as computer-assisted steering that relates to road speed rather than engine speed, automatic gearbox controlled by a 32-bit processor, instrument panel that gives warnings and trip information in eleven languages, and anti-lock ABS braking that uses sensors at each wheel to detect differences in rotational speed.

The external styling was developed under the guidance of Chief Stylist Geoff Lawson and honours Jaguar styling legacy whilst setting an assertive

new design course, although the XK8 bears more than a passing resemblance to both the E-Type and the prototype XJ13 prototype whilst adopting the benefits of the latest aerodynamic developments.

The XJ Series was continued in 1997 with the introduction of the XJ8 marque, available in 3.2-litre Sport as well as 3.2- and 4.0-litre Classic versions, which upon their introduction carried price tags of £35,180, £36,380 and £41,880 respectively.

The XJ8 features advanced electronics that allow the controls for powertrain and chassis to 'communicate' with each other thus enabling

In the new XJR, Jaguar was the first modern motor manufacturer to introduce a supercharged engine into a luxury saloon. Faster than many sports cars, the marque is instantly recognizable for its wire-mesh grille.

optimization of performance, efficiency and safety; also of note is the automatic transmission which is factory-filled for the life of its transmission, and the camshafts that are driven by zero-maintenance chains.

In common with other marques in the modern Jaguar range, the models are bestowed with an abundance of technologically advanced features whilst retaining traditional quality furnishings and elegance. The 4.0-litre XJ8 possesses sports alloy wheels, electrically adjustable front seats and headrests, and electronic traction control as standard, whilst also featuring the advanced Variable Cam Phasing system for optimization of engine power.

JAGUAR
4882 NT
JAG 1

Fifty years of XK Sportsters, represented here by the XK120, XK140, XK150, XKSS and XKR, evoke many memories and recall many proud moments.

Building on the success of the XK8, the XKR Coupé (pictured) and Convertible made their debuts in 1996, and the marque is now the fastest selling mainstream production car in Jaguar's history.

In 1998 the cruise control switching and stereo buttons were moved to the steering wheel for easier access, and other interior revisions included a revised instrument panel with new gauges, analogue clock, and trip omputer.

Jaguar's new high-performance XKR Coupé and Convertible sports cars were unveiled at the Geneva Motor Show in March 1998. Building on the success of the XK8 now the best-selling sports car in Jaguar's history, with sales of over 14,500 in 1997 the XKR is destined to carry the range through the last years of the 1990s and into the next century.

Powered by the 4.0-litre supercharged AJ-V8 engine that produces an exhilarating 370bhp, both the Coupé and Convertible models are capable of

0-60 in 5.2 and 5.4 seconds respectively and have a top speed of 155mph, factors that make the XKR the fastest mainstream production Jaguar to date. The five-speed electronically controlled automatic transmission provides exceedingly smooth running whilst also benefiting fuel economy, and the advanced design of the engine ensures that the XKR meets current EU emissions requirements as well as those proposed for the year 2000. Jaguar has modified the suspension, steering, braking and tyre systems, and the XKR includes as standard the CATS system, although improved over that incorporated in the XJR.

The XKR embodies the award-winning style of the XK8 in its elegant

On-Board Diagnosis

Jaguar cars' electrical systems are carefully designed for reliability, and the company employs an enhanced version of Ford's FDS2000 service diagnostic computer on its production line and in dealerships worldwide to ensure that fault-finding is as accurate as possible. The Jaguar Diagnostic System is able to interrogate all the car's systems and plot a step-by-step path through the fault-finding process. An electrical current probe measures the currents flowing through components, whilst the measurement probe is able to simulate some switched functions and also take voltage measurements. The Portable Diagnostic Link can be connected to the car under driving conditions, and can detect any fault that lasts for more than one tenth of a second!

and powerful flowing lines that evoke the sports car legends of the past the XK120 and C- and D-Types as well as the E-Type and the traditional Jaguar oval air intake mouth features a bright mesh stainless-steel grille that emphasizes its family links with the XJR. The colour range is limited to eight colours that include the new Phoenix Red that was especially selected to suit the sporting character of these new models.

Although 1998 prices for the Coupé and Convertible were £59,300 and £66,300 respectively, these figures were considerably lower than those of comparable models by other manufacturers.Fifty years before, Jaguar had launched the XK120 which itself set new performance standards in its own time. Commenting on the launch of the XKR, Nick Scheele, Chairman and Chief Executive of Jaguar said: 'XKR provides an unrivalled blend of styling panache, supercar performance, handling precision and outstanding value for money. This year Jaguar celebrates the fiftieth anniversary of the launch of the brilliant XK120 ... XKR is a worthy descendant which I am sure will further enhance the reputation and appeal of the XK8 range among motoring enthusiasts worldwide'.

Although comprehensive details were not available at the time of writing, Jaguar was scheduled to build its new S-Type saloon (code-named X200) at Castle Bromwich for release in October 1998, and reportedly featuring the all-alloy AJ26 V8 engine of 3.2-litre (225bhp) and 4.0-litre (275bhp) displacements. Competing against models of the calibre of the BMW 5 Series, the first all-new Jaguar to be established under Ford's ownership was due to be launched at the NEC Motor Show in Birmingham in October 1998, with showroom models available in March 1999.

And no doubt it will be welcomed with the same measure of acclaim that has greeted so many of the outstanding and innovative models produced by a company that celebrates its own eightieth anniversary just beyond the turn of the century.

The cockpit of the XKR is available in this classic configuration with the traditional leather and veneers, or can be ordered with the 'sport' interior which features black leather and black dash board.